From Beauty Fear
to Beauty Fever

ASIAN THOUGHT AND CULTURE

Sandra A. Wawrytko
General Editor

Vol. 67

PETER LANG
New York • Washington, D.C./Baltimore • Bern
Frankfurt • Berlin • Brussels • Vienna • Oxford

Xin Yang

From Beauty Fear to Beauty Fever

A Critical Study of Contemporary Chinese Female Writers

PETER LANG
New York • Washington, D.C./Baltimore • Bern
Frankfurt • Berlin • Brussels • Vienna • Oxford

Library of Congress Cataloging-in-Publication Data

Yang, Xin.
From beauty fear to beauty fever: a critical study of contemporary
Chinese female writers / Xin Yang.
p. cm. — (Asian thought and culture; v. 67)
Includes bibliographical references and index.
1. Chinese literature—Women authors—History and criticism.
2. Chinese literature—21st century—History and criticism. 3. Feminine beauty
(Aesthetics) in literature. 4. Mian, Mian—Criticism and interpretation.
5. Wei Hui—Criticism and interpretation. I. Title.
PL2278.Y37   895.1'352099287—dc22   2010046755
ISBN 978-1-4331-1131-0
ISSN 0893-6870

Bibliographic information published by **Die Deutsche Nationalbibliothek.**
Die Deutsche Nationalbibliothek lists this publication in the "Deutsche
Nationalbibliografie"; detailed bibliographic data is available
on the Internet at http://dnb.d-nb.de/.

The paper in this book meets the guidelines for permanence and durability
of the Committee on Production Guidelines for Book Longevity
of the Council of Library Resources.

© 2011 Peter Lang Publishing, Inc., New York
29 Broadway, 18th floor, New York, NY 10006
www.peterlang.com

Printed in Germany

TABLE OF CONTENTS

ACKNOWLEDGMENTS

I wish to express sincere appreciation to Professors Wendy Larson, Tze-lan Sang, Maram Epstein, and Kathleen R Karlyn for their assistance in the preparation of this manuscript. For years, Professor Larson has gaven me much-needed insightful suggestions on how to be a scholar. She is a true mentor who leads me to my own scholary space. She not only guided me through the project, but also painstakingly edited my manuscript. Professor Sang has shared her knowledge of Chinese culture with me and constantly encouraged me to be on the right track. Professor Epstein's critical comments always pushed me to think through the argument. Professor Karlyn's profound understanding of literary and feminist theories always attracted my admiration. I am greatly indebted to them all for their years of patience with me.

Many thanks are also due to my colleagues, friends and family who have given me thoughtful comments, intellectural inspiration, constant encouagement and emotional support. Their understanding has been greatly encouraging for me.

This project was supported in part by a grant from the Center for the Study of Women in Society at the University of Oregon in 2003. My field trip to China would not have been smooth without this source of financial assistance.

Finally, I dedicate the book to my generation: we have come a long way to realize what we are and who we are.

INTRODUCTION

This book examines the mass consumption of "beauty" (female writers) and "writing" (texts) in China at the turn of the 21ˢᵗ century. The so-called beauty writers (*meinü zuojia*), famous or infamous, created a visual spectacle through their writing and beautiful images. Driven by both self-expression and marketing, their novels, typically semi-autobiographical, were either seen as providing a new kind of literature or dismissed as mere commercial pulp fiction. They also constituted in themselves an interesting social phenomenon.

When I decided to write on this sensational though brief literary and social event, I was already "out of fashion," for by this time, the beauty writers have become naturalized as the accepted majority, have changed their writing styles, or have slipped into oblivion. Their initial stunning cultural images and literary reputations have become more and more obscure in the public eye. How did the beauty writer, a hot phenomenon in fin-de-siècle China, quickly become passé? Are beauty writers like any fashion, as quick to come as to go? Or have they suffered the fate of all beauties once they are no longer young and beautiful?

Wang Yuan, a woman urban fiction writer born in the 1960s, jokingly remarked, "If somebody were to call me a beauty writer, I would be extremely angry. But if people call me a beauty, I would be extremely happy." She added, "Female writers born in the 1970s have been 'codified' (*fuhao hua*). 'Beauty' has been regarded as the trademark of their writings, and that is what made them famous. Ours (novels by writers born in the 60s) do not possess such a trademark."[1]

If the female writers born in the 70s have indeed been codified as beauties, what does it mean that "beauty" should have come to dominate public discourse in a country where physical attractiveness had for so long been regarded as the residue of feudalism and foreign imperialism? What impact did such beauty writing have on China's cultural scene in general and Chinese literature in particular? Were these high-profile women writers empowered by the challenge to conventional morality which they represented? Or were they objectified by a voyeuristic gaze as they moved to sell their attractiveness in the market? More broadly, what does the beauty writer, as both a cultural and literary phenomenon, tell us about shifts in the gender power balance?

In my book, I propose to read the born-in-the-70s female writers as both a literary and social text.[2] I argue that the textual representation and market packaging of the beauty writer plays on the boundary between elitist literature and popular culture, subverting the conventional image and definition of a writer/intellectual and actualizing the personal/national fantasy of wealth-pursuit and identity establishment. The textual profile of the unconventional women represents both a cultural ideal and a cultural dilemma that corresponds to the social reality of the turn of the 21st century, and provides a vehicle for both writers and readers to participate in the imagination of a new global citizen in China. Once writers had fully absorbed and manipulated the transnational imagination constructed in their texts, they started to return to more indigenous cultural forms. Such a self-promoting high profile female writer and her unconventional text challenged the dominant moral and ethical thinking, and brought into popular conversation controversial views both from the market itself as well as from literary critics. Although when writing and the pretty face combine to become a form of capital, and to possess a distinct exchange value, enmeshing the writer in the parochial/global patriarchal order, she nonetheless speaks in her own voice; she is by no means a mere passive, silent subject.

Defining the "Newly-new Generation" (*xinxin renlei*)

Beauty writers, or glam-lit writers, first emerged in literary journals in the category of "writers born in the 1970s," or "post-70s," and were addressed in general as the "Newly-new generation" (*xinxin renlei*) to distinguish them from the "new generation" which referred to a generation who never suffered from the pain and poverty of the war. Taiwan employed the term to describe its own rebellious youngsters born between 1965 and 1975.[3] "New generation writer" in Mainland China denoted, rather loosely, a group of urban-based writers born in the 1960s, such as Zhu Wen, Qiu Huadong, He Dun, Han Dong, Chen Ran and Lin Bai. Sometimes it also included Zhang Xianliang, Liu Suola, Mo Yan and other new voices who experimented with new writing styles and narrative subjects in the late 1980s and early 1990s.[4] Younger writers, born in the 1970s were, thus, "newly new."

In February 1996, a non-official literary journal *Black and Blue* (Hei lan) first raised the concept of "post-seventies." Chen Wei, founder of the journal, hoped *Black and Blue* could be a "pure literature" (*chun wenxue*) journal contributed by "writing fellows" (*xiezuo ren*).[5] It happened that all the authors in the inaugural issue were born in the 1970s, and Chen denominated them "Chinese writers born after 1970."[6]

Many critics, such as Li Jingze (1997), Ge Hongbing (2001) and Xie You-shun (2003), have attempted to characterize this Newly-new generation as belonging to a transitional generation. Without the dramatic experience of the revolution and social turmoil, they had grown up during the period when China was opening to the outside world and engaging in economic reform. Though at school, they had been educated within the framework of orthodox socialist ideologies, they were also exposed to foreign commodities and an increasingly commercialized world, reaching their twenties in the mid- and late-1990s, where a new generation was attempting to establish itself in the fast-changing post-socialist scene by ridiculing and subverting older institutions.

Though *Black and Blue* only survived for one issue, its post-70s concept was appropriated by various official or formal literary journals, newspaper and websites, suggesting a new generation that had started to speak in its unique voice in the public forums. Literary journals such as *Xiaoshuo jie* (Fiction World), *Furong* (Hibiscus), *Zuojia* (Writer), *Changcheng* (Great Wall), *Shanhua* (Mountain flower), *Shouhuo* (Harvest), and *Zhongshan* (Zhong Mountain) opened special columns. *Xiaoshuo jie* launched a "post-seventies" column. *Furong* started "people born in the seventies" and "Reshape post-seventies." *Zuojia* highlighted a special issue on "female writers born in the seventies." *Changcheng* presented "works of people born in the seventies." *Shanhua* presented "writers born in the seventies." *Shouhuo, Renming wenxue* (People's literature), and *Zhongshan* also published novels written by this group of writers.

Among the many "Seventies" columns, female writers occupied a dominant position. In the winter of 1997, Zong Renfa, the editor-in-chief of *Writer*, Shi Zhanjun, a literary critic and researcher at Shandong University, and Li Jingze, the vice editor-in-chief of *People's Literature* announced that there was "something new in the air," and after an exciting "conspiracy" (*mimou*), decided to bring the new literary trend to light in the special issue of *Writer* where the female writers born in the 70s made their collective debut. As the three male intellectuals expected, female writers' different visual/textual self-representations created quite a sensation. The term *meinü zuojia*, or "beauty writer," first used by Wei Hui in this issue, also became a hot word for the media.[7]

These female writers born in the 1970s share some similarities. They were in their twenties when they were most active in writing fiction at the turn of the millennium. They were well-educated city-dwellers, producing predominantly urban fiction. Their semi-autobiographical protagonists are, unsurprisingly, young urban women engaged in intense self-discovery in cosmopolitan cities. Sex and desire were no longer taboo, and when it came to literary (self) promotion, their beautiful images formed the focus of their marketing strategy.

The collocation "beauty/writer" is bizarre, yet symbolic in important ways. First, the term implies a blurring of the boundary between literary writing proper and popular fiction.[8] The Chinese term *zuojia* (writer) implies a sense of the elite, a person who is literarily engaged. Yet *meinü* (beauty) seems erotic and vulgarized. On the one hand, beauty writers' novels are packaged like other commodities, and the writers' attractiveness is sold. On the other hand, both the writers and their writings have succeeded in drawing the attention of mainstream literary and academic critics. Mian Mian's novel *Candy*, for example, was first published in *Shouhuo* (Harvest), an elite literary journal.[9] In 2001, the editorial committee to choose "the fifty most important Chinese novels," which is composed of six well-established scholars, writers and literary critics, announced that beauty writers had "become one important trend in China," along with other well-established literary movements such as "root searching," "avant-garde" and the "new realism."[10] Therefore, the emergence of beauty writers extended the conception of *zuojia* from the intellectual and the academic to the arenas of mass consumption and entertainment.

Second, the combination of "beauty" and "writer" indicates that women's social roles are sometimes consciously or unconsciously related to eroticism, in a playful way. Beauty becomes both cultural property and marketing strategy. It is a common practice for the publishers and mass media to showcase female writers' "artistic pictures" (*yishu zhao*) on their books or along with their novels published in journals. After all, a female beauty is expected to catch the public attention. A female writer with a beautiful appearance is more likely to create a sensation that the market would like to see.

Gender Power behind the Beauty Culture

The beauty culture has been a controversial issue in the eyes of feminists and critics for years. The controversies focus on whether beautification empowers or oppresses women. Simone de Beauvoir and art historian John Berger's "other" theories have played an important role in analyzing power relations as concerns the issue of beauty. By studying visual images in painting and mass media, John Berger concludes that the male gaze, directed at women, has become a principle of visual organization.[11] Simone de Beauvoir suggests that "He is the Subject, he is the Absolute — she is the Other."[12] She holds that women's appearance always depends on attracting the attention of another and women appraise themselves through male eyes.[13] De Beauvoir argues that the patriarchal institutions place certain expectations on women and prescribe women's social and personal images. Men control most social institutions and expect women to be beautiful and desirable, and women to beautify their bodies to meet men's expectations. A woman's beautification, therefore, subjugates her to patriarchal ideology and institutions. Following this logic, early Second Wave feminists are seen "as enemies of the stiletto heel and beauty parlor."[14]

Naomi Wolf, for instance, strongly attacks beauty culture. She sees a "beauty myth" behind women's constant desire to improve their body image. The myth, Wolf suggests, is nothing other than male-dominated capitalism. Wolf carefully examines various realms in which the beauty myth has its impact on a woman's job, life, and health. "Beauty" in the modern age in the West, Wolf declares, "is the last, best belief system that keeps male dominance intact. In assigning value to women in a vertical hierarchy according to a culturally imposed physical standard, it is an expression of power relations in which women must unnaturally compete for resources that men have appropriated for themselves."[15] One example Wolf gives is the image of beauty in the mass media, one of the various destructive social controls. Constantly seeing unusually beautiful images, women then feel insecure about their bodies and subject themselves to the exploitation of various industries such as the cosmetics and diet industries.[16]

This kind of (male) subject/(female) object framework is a powerful discourse through which to investigate the gender power balance. Yet it is inadequate to explain the fact that men are also gazed at by women and that men also are subject to social expectations. Efrat Tseëlon does not quite agree with the "the looker-subject" and "the looked-object" pattern. She directs attention to Mead (1934) and Sartre (1943/1966), who note that everybody, male and female alike, depends on the other's acknowledgement, *he* and *she* are mutually evaluating each other. Tseëlon studies the beauty scenario from the perspective of "cultural psychology" and suggests a dialectical relation between the looker and the looked:

> The argument equating gaze with masculine position and power is problematic. In the distinction between the man "who is doing the gaze" and the women who is the object of the gaze there is an assumption that one position, that of the onlooker, is inherently more powerful than the other. However, a careful examination of the use of "invisible" and "visible" shows them to encompass a dialectical rather than a unilateral meaning. "Invisible" as ignored and trivialized is powerless. But invisible as the source of gaze (that is, the one who is looking without being looked at) is powerful. Similarly, visible as objectified is powerless, but visible as prominent and dominant is powerful.[17]

She proposes that "women are always on a stage, always observed, always visible: they lack a back region both literally and symbolically."[18] In Tseëlon's framework, women perform for the male audience. Yet the fact that they are prominent and visible on the stage does not mean that they are totally power-less. If a woman knows how to take advantage of her visible, to-be-gazed-at po-sition, she can be a powerful figure.

The visible/invisible pattern is very pertinent to the highly visible "beauty writers" and their attractive (self) representation in the media. Though it was male intellectuals/editors who brought to light the young female writers in a way that was more or less related to sensationalist pursuit, female writers also aggressively cooperated with the media, presenting themselves as the beautiful new humanity. They actively promoted the beauty discourse, which extended gender politics and the power balance beyond the "male/onlooker" and "female/object" pattern. Wei Hui, for instance, was highly aware of stylish fashion. She said, "With a blue printed *qipao*, I think I can transform myself from a *linglei* (unconventional) writer to a mainstream beauty."[19] In her essay on how she wrote novels, she was quite proud of her life as a new urbanite with "metal-color makeup."[20] She even designed the cover image of her book *Shanghai Baby*, which is her own picture. It is true that female writers were gazed at, objectified and commodified once they were in the spotlight of the attention. Yet I do not quite agree with Li Jingze's point that the ubiquitous beauty writers epitomize the derogation of women's status in general.[21] In fact, visibility and public attention was what female writers enthusiastically pursued, and glamorousness was what they actively promoted.

Female writers' self promotion of glamour sent a stunning and shocking message to the public. People questioned the morality of these writers and accused them of exchanging good looks for fame and profit. Male writer Qiu Huadong's novel "Xin meiren" (New beauty), for instance, elucidates the symbolic meaning of aggressive beautiful women. Qiu in his novel portrayed a dangerous femme fatal in the new urban condition. The female character is an artist, also one of many "new beauties" who target those financially successful American, Japanese, and transnational investors in the cosmopolitan city. She uses her pretty face and tempting body, takes advantage not only of the Chinese male narrator, but also a rich Japanese businessman and then a French artist, and eventually becomes a successful painter. In the transnational competition for capital and woman, the Chinese man is defeated.[22] The term "beauty" obviously suggests the role that a pretty face plays in a woman's social mobility. The attractive novelists in reality, like the good-looking artist in Qiu's story, caused a similar anxiety, especially when the displaying of a pretty face was in the literary world, formerly a sacred and sublime area. The most common moral condemnation denounced beauty writers as "decadent" and "rotten," and pandering to the vulgar taste of the market.[23] Because of this, most of the female writers strongly rejected the label. Mian Mian, Zhao Bo and Zhou Jieru, for example, claimed that they had nothing to do with beauty, that what they were doing was serious literary creation.

Beauty, historically speaking, was not a negative word in China's context. A brief glance at pre-modern Chinese literary history brings us many beauties depicted in poems, essays, drama and novels written by male writers: a country girl who works in the field (Luo Fu, "Xianghe qu"), a woman warrior who fights in the battlefield (Hua Mulan, "Mulan ci"), concubines who sacrifice their bodies for the nation and political struggles, and literary courtesans who befriend scholars were all appreciated and admired as legendary beauties. Nevertheless, in these cases, it was male literati who textually constructed these images of beauty. A beautiful woman was constructed to represent certain cultural ideals, and different types of beauties fitted into men's various fantasies about women. Men depicted women as pure, brave, culturally-refined, self-sacrificing or sexually appealing. At the end of the twentieth century, however, it was the woman herself who explored her own subjectivity and represented herself as an attractive figure in her literary engagement. Though she was also partially manipulated by the capitalism, her active promotion of her own self was to some extent threatening, as she empowered herself by speaking in her own voice and also becoming commercially successful.

Interestingly, though most female writers rejected the title of beauty writers, they nevertheless took delight in being beautiful women. When Ellen Zetzel Lambert addresses the beauty issue from a personal and subjective position, she argues that it is a feminist issue that beautiful appearances not only do but should matter. "It matters just because outward beauty is the expression of the inner self, because it is the bearer of identity." She believed that "it is a very basic need for an adult, as for a child, to be loved in the body; and as feminists we are mistaken in denying the validity of that need."[24] Though the beautiful representation of self is a way of self-expression, the "inner self," nevertheless, is highly subjective. Lambert admits that the "beauty question is inherently problematic, not because the criteria for beauty are subjective and thus difficult to define, but because the question of beauty's status cannot finally be adjudicated." Yet she emphasizes that her primary interest is the "subjective experience of beauty."[25]

Embracing beauty, make-up and traditional femininity is also part of the third-wave feminists' larger agenda of recognizing hybridity, contradiction, differences, multiple possibilities of oppression and powers.[26] Feminism's third wave "contains elements of second-wave critique of beauty culture, sexual abuse, and power structures while it also acknowledges and makes use of the pleasure, danger and defining power of those structures."[27] As Jennifer Baumgardner and Amy Richards argue: "Feminism isn't about what choice you make but the freedom to make that choice."[28] The female writers certainly had enjoyed the freedom of self-fashioning, though the freedom itself involves the paradox of both visibility and objectification.

The booming beauty discourse in *fin de siècle* China unfolded against and through modern social, cultural and historical contexts. After years of revolutionary policies of "gender erasure," "beauty fever" was the product of the intertwined narratives of resistance politics, feminism, capitalism, consumerism, and the postmodern ludic carnival: the issue that I will elucidate in Chapter One.[29] Because of these narratives, the social symbolic value of beauty writers is as important as, if not more important than, their literary meaning. In this book, I will take an interdisciplinary approach to critique the "beauty writer" phenomenon and examine the intertextuality between literary genres and the social engagement.

Beauty Plus Writing: Writing Goes Visual in the Global Context

When talking about her generation's writing, Wei Wei said,

> We live in the city and do whatever is related to "writing a novel." We read the best foreign novels, face everything the information age brings to us, and confront the clash of modernization... It is very easy for us to begin and imitate writing. We change "Paris" into "Beijing," "George" into "Li Ming." [30]

"George" is a typical name in translated foreign novels and "Li Ming" a common Chinese name. According to Wei Wei, her generation began writing by imitating the general format and content of foreign novels with slight modifications to adjust to the local situation. As for her own literary activity, Wei Wei explained, "I have piles of foreign novels on my bookshelf and in my bed, in translated versions or in the original language. They are the source of our Chinese writing."[31]

Wei Wei's words described her generation's writing in Chinese in the global context in the late 1990s, when the foreign imagination provided the initial inspiration for the urban-based Newly-new generation. Li Jingze once commented with playfully sarcastic tone, "For the seventies female writers, they know more about what is happening in Paris than what is happening around them."[32] From Wei Hui's endless references to Western high- and low-cultural texts, Mian Mian's seeking of salvation in rock'n'roll, and Zhou Jieru's infatuation with cyberspace, we can see that the foreign and distant "other" offers insight into their local lifestyle and occupies a dominant position in their textual imagination. In their writings, the transnational cultural imagination, with its brand-name commodities and global travel, became a tempting lifestyle, in which writers were the cool urbanites who blissfully consumed the city. The fiction expresses the public frenzy to identify with the new, exotic, global opportunities.

Most of the writings of this group of female writers has an "I" as the narrator and the main protagonist. The writer's self and her subjective experience make up the majority of the texts. The story line and how the writer writes novels are intertwined, turning the writing into meta-fiction and the story into semi-autobiography. Mian Mian's *Candy*, Zhou Jieru's *Xiao Yao's Net* and Wei Hui's *Shanghai Baby* (Shanghai baobei), "Crazy Like Wei Hui" (Xiang Wei Hui yiyang fengkuang) and "Pistol of Desire" (Yuwang shouqiang), to name a few, are all about how a woman protagonist works on a writing project and eventually becomes a writer.

Gayle Greene examines novels written by Erica Jong, Gail Godwin, Doris Lessing and several others in the 1960s and 1970s, and reads their writings as "feminist metafiction:" a woman writing about a woman's writing. Greene reads the feminist metafiction as resistance to the established literary conventions, such as the "happy-ever-after" myth, defined by male canonical writers.[33] "The writing on writing" in these Chinese female writers' textual practices certainly subverted the sublime myth of writing. Ever since the beginning of the twentieth century, Liang Qichao positioned *xiaoshuo* (fiction) as an important part of the grand mission of transforming and educating people. Writers have also been equated with intellectuals who shoulder the lofty responsibilities of liberation and education.[34] Nevertheless, the new forces of mass culture have challenged this elitism. The seventies female writers are a good example. While they develop a storyline, they also tell readers how they write the novel. They show less interest in serving the grand social, intellectual or aesthetic goals of literature than in articulating and fulfilling various personal and pragmatic desires. Mian Mian noted that writing entered her life like a doctor, to cure her mental and psychological trauma. Wei Hui said, "I write only because I want to possess several beautiful books before I am old."[35] For her, writing is one of many stylish professions in the cosmopolitan space. Writing, as it has been constructed and deconstructed in the text, becomes a game, a cool urban profession, a self-healing process and a self-absorbed adventure.

Furthermore, to bring out their personal experience and individual desires, these writers adopted, or partially adopted, the first-person voice. The overlapping experience of the protagonists and the writer herself turn the stories into half autobiography and half fiction. The playfully blurred boundary between the real and the unreal, as Lori Saint-Martin argues, is one strategy for women to explore their sexuality and transgress the confining confessional framework.[36]

Saint-Martin is one of many scholars who have examined the reading of women's private narratives in Europe and North America.[37] Irene Gammel regards women's sexual self-representation, embodied through life writing such as the diary and the journal as well as the popular media, such as TV talk show, as a discursive practice related to the Western tradition of confessional politics.[38] By examining both "confessional writing" and "confessional reading," Gammel shows that women's sexual re-presentation is constantly appropriated and reshaped so that it fits into the male's version of female sexuality. Confessional reading often omits the transgressive elements and celebrates the traditional institutions. In this way, women's voices of sexuality are not silenced, but rather tamed and re-colonized to fit patriarchal frames of references.[39]

Yet women employed various strategies to disrupt the confessional politics as a tool of social policing. One strategy is the writing of "confessional fiction," as Lori Saint-Martin terms it, the most personal and intimate details of an author's life in the form of fiction. Confessional fiction, with its hybrid of fiction and autobiography, provides "a safe space for women to explore their sexuality while both enabling and disrupting a reading of the text as autobiography." Confessional fiction also protects writers as dangerous subjects, as it invites *literal* readings of the texts.[40]

Lori Saint-Martin situates the transgressive nature of confessional fiction in Catholic Québec. Though the sexual self-representation in the mixed genre of fiction and nonfiction would probably still provoke a voyeuristic peek, women nevertheless playfully manipulate the personal secrets on a literary level and ridicule the policing power of confession. The novels of Chinese female writers are not confessional in nature; writers' playing with reality and fiction, however, certainly created an active female subjectivity and challenged the patriarchal concepts of both women and women writers. The daring self-representation, the narrative of female bodies, and the tell-all politics turned female writers into highly visible, yet controversial, figures. Their active maintenance of the high-profile image of the media star also differentiated them from their counterparts in the previous generation: they not only voiced themselves verbally, but also promoted themselves visually.

The (self) representation of the female writers projected an alternative literary image that played a considerable part in selling the texts. Their high-profile public images as glamorous stars were one of many increasingly popular visualized texts in the cultural market. As picture books, films, and TV programs provided alternative ways for people to consume stories, entertainment and knowledge, "Reading visual images" (*du tu*) came into competition with the conventional way of "reading characters." Taiwanese cartoonist Cai Zhizhong, for instance, adapted many traditional Chinese philosophical texts of Confucius, Zhuangzi, and Laozi into cartoon books, which sold very well in mainland China. Books such as *Lao zhaopian* (Old pictures) and an "Old Shanghai" memoir series also have pictures occupying a considerable part of the book's content.[41] These picture-dominated books recount early twentieth century Chinese history through nostalgic images. In 1999, Yang Xiaoyan uses the word "image-reading era" (*dutu shidai*) to address the power of the visual culture in changing the reading habits of the public.[42] In the commercial economy, it is an important marketing strategy to attract consumers' attention. Visualized history, philosophy and memory offered people an easy alternative way to consume culture, and also provided the profitable attention that publishers would like to see. Therefore, female writers' writing as a literary and social text was a manifestation of the heightened emphasis on the visual, an expression of the intensified levels of commodification generated by global capitalism. However, this is not to say that Chinese print culture is diminishing. On the contrary, it is invigorated with the input of the visual. To examine the visualized literary moment, I make use of Roland Barthes' notion of texts, which includes both visual and verbal communicative systems. [43] I will employ both novels and journal photos as the target texts for critical analysis.

Structure

Seventies female writers were by no means a homogenous group, though they were always grouped under the over-simplified categories of "seventies" or "beauty." There were sub groups of "problem girls" such as Mian Mian, stylish "bad girls" represented by Wei Hui, and elegant "petit bourgeois" women like Anni Baobei and Zhao Bo. Additionally, there were also writers whose focus was beyond the dazzlingly new cityscape. Jin Renshun, who debuted along with other female writers, for instance, depicted the violent reality of rural youngsters suffering from poverty in her novella "The Young Schoolmates" (Qia tongxue shaonian). Zhu Wenying wrote about small Jiangnan area towns, as well as the emotional subtlety of the small town residents in stories such as "Floating Life" (Fu sheng). Dai Lai focused her attention on the listless life of ordinary people in small cities in "Are You Ready" (Zhunben hao le ma).

Different critics, journal editors and website columns also have different recognitions of glam-lit writers. For instance, Shao Yanjun categorized Wei Hui, Mian Mian, Chun Shu and Zhang Yueran in her *"Meinü wenxue" xianxiang yanjiu* (Study of the "beauty literature" phenomenon).[44] Whereas in *Shi da meinu zuojia piping shu* (Criticizing ten beauty writers), a popular text, the author Ta Ai (He Loves) put Wei Hui, Mian Mian, Sheng Keyi, Chun Shu, Anni Baobei, Jiu Dan, Yin Lichuan, Hong Yin, Zhao Nin and Muzi Mei into the category of beauty writers.[45]

In my study, I use five perspectives to approach the beauty writer phenomenon: historical image, youthful time, literary space, alternative writing and body narrative, which are related to different aspects of the social and cultural scenarios at the turn of the century. The writers whom I have chosen were very active figures between 1997 and 2003 on both literary and popular levels: Mian Mian, Zhou Jieru, Anni Baobei, Wei Hui and Muzi Mei. Other figures are also included to help flesh out the historical and theoretical background. Though Anni Baobei and Muzi Mei did not debut with the other female writers, their fame, which began on the Internet, turned them into late-comers in the "seventies" category. Although Muzi Mei is not a novelist per se, her story exemplifies an extreme case of "body writing." My book tries to capture controversial moments and bring them into academic focus. It is my goal to use their cases to provide multiple perspectives on the sensational beauty writer phenomenon.

Chapter One provides a historical account against which the beauty dis-course comes into being. It focuses on the construction of femininity in the media and in literary spaces. Female writers emerged first as part of the "born-in-the-70s writer" category. Yet gradually their hyper-visibility outshone their male contemporaries, partly as a result of the long term repression of beautiful femininity in the revolutionary era, and partly as the new energy of commer-cialization. Chapter Two examines the construction of "time," and the form-ing of subgroup youth as it is represented in Mian Mian's writings. Born in the seventies, female writers became most active in the late nineties. The issue of youth is related to *time* and *timing*, as I will demonstrate, which makes glam-lit writers both a literary coincidence and a historical continuity. Chapter Three looks into the spaces female writers explore for their expression. Urban-based, female writers catch the high-tech trend and expand their literary space to the Internet. The urban/virtual reality, in the context of China at the turn of the century, constitutes a new escapist imagination in female writers' literary en-gagement. The dialectical relation between the urban and cyberpace is best embodied in Zhou Jieru and Anni Baobei's writings. Chapter Four scrutinizes the writing itself by doing an inter-textual reading of Wei Hui, the most de-monized female writer, and her novels. Wei Hui subverted the conventional images of a writer and turned writing into one of many stylish urban engage-ments. Writing as a form of elite culture gave way to postmodern lightheart-edness. Chapter Five is on the "body writing" paradigm, which has been closely related to glam-lit writers. The writer in question is Muzi Mei. Though not a real writer per se, Muzi Mei epitomizes how far body writing can go. By examining different interpretations of the body writing concept, I will do a feminist critique of the violence of the patriarchal discourses in facing the prospering female narrative.

In the 21st century, "beauty fever" persists. Though the sensational moment of female writers is vanishing, the beauty discourse that they started and popularized has been gradually mainstreamed and naturalized. More and more beauty-related words have been invented: beauty entrepreneur, beauty athlete, and beauty politician, to name a few. Though facing the patriarchal appropriation of various terms, female writers nevertheless initiated an alternative female narrative *within* the patriarchal framework. However controversial they were, female writers brought people's attention to a new discourse and aesthetic in 1990s' China. My book will extend beyond their glamorous veneer and explore their historical continuity with the rest of contemporary Chinese literature.

CHAPTER ONE

From Invisibility to Hyper-Visibility: Constructing Femininity in the Media and Literary Space

Beauty, in the second half of the twentieth century, was part of the social construction of femininity. From the 1940s to the 1990s, China witnessed a development from "beauty fear" to "beauty fever." The change was closely related to shifts in China's national politics in different historical periods. Beauty fear resulted from the revolutionary ambition of denouncing the old institutionalized ideologies and embracing gender equality. Beauty fever was driven by commercialization in the mid- and late 1990s, when the global/local, or "glocal" as it is called by Roland Robertson, became the new social reality and broke the boundaries of world/China, official/folk, and elite/mass.[1] The changing ideology had a direct impact on the (self) representation of feminine beauty in the mass media and literature. Femininity, which had been constructed in the Maoist era as tough and strong, underwent another round of reconstruction during the reform period.

The goal of Chapter One is to trace the historical background against which the discourse of the "beauty writer" emerged. The reason that I want to focus on both the literature and the media is because almost all of the seventies female writers worked closely with the media. They published their novels both in literary journals and magazines, as well as on the Internet. The literary sensation that the beauty writers created, to a large extent, was realized through the ubiquitous, sensation-seeking media.

Why was "beauty" plus "writer" such a big issue? Why did writers' femininity play an important part in their literary engagement? The significance of beauty writers should be viewed against the backdrop of China's changing ideologies on femininity. In this chapter, I will first sketch the historical construction of femininity and then focus on *Writer*, a literary journal where seventies female writers made their collective debut.[2] Partly manipulated by the media and the consumer market, and partly driven by female writers' self-expression, attractive femininity became a trademark of the new generation authors, and also enabled female writers to outshine their male contemporaries and to stand out as the glamorous writer-cum-stars.

Examining the Invisibility of Feminine Beauty

In 1961, Mao Zedong, the revolutionary leader, wrote a poem and enthusiastically praised women who resolutely abandoned material accessories and became revolutionary soldiers:

> Early rays of sun illumine the parade grounds
> and these handsome girls heroic in the wind,
>   with rifles five feet long.
> Daughters of China with a marvelous will,
> you prefer hardy uniforms to colorful silk.[3]

In this poem, Mao took up the position of the father and encouraged his daughters to be high-spirited warriors. In reality, Chinese women followed the revolutionary guidelines and hid their feminine traits in order to demonstrate their revolutionary passion and conformity to Party doctrine. Their bodies disappeared in baggy clothes and dull-colored uniforms. They became the "iron women," tough and strong.

Ideologically speaking, the iron women derived from the ambitious, revolutionary utopian plan to realize gender equality. The 1950 New Marriage Law and the 1954 Constitution officially guaranteed women equality and basic legal rights. The official rhetoric proclaimed that "men and women are equal;" and "women hold half of the sky." Women were encouraged to merge themselves into the "ocean of the collective" and contribute to the cause of socialism.

A close examination of this equality reveals problems. What's the standard of equality? As Varda Burstyn explains:

> The notion of equality for women...implicitly but firmly sets the lifeways and goals of masculine existence as the standards to which women should aspire and against which official estimates of their "progress" will be made. It poses the problem as women's "catching up to men," rather than as a problem for women and men to solve together by changing the conditions and relations of their shared lives — from their intimate to their large-scale social interaction.[4]

The so-called collectivity was actually male collectivism, which was systematically established by men in light of masculine standards. Male discourse was naturalized, legitimized, and internalized into the political system, cultural mechanisms, and moral judgments. The official rhetoric of gender equality implied that women should identify with revolutionized patriarchal standards and the social, political, and cultural systems defined by men. The slogans declaring that "women can do whatever men can do," and "man and woman are alike," as noted feminist Li Xiaojiang points out, actually "relinquished the category of women." [5] The result of gender equality was women's acceptance of an institutionalized masculine aesthetic, as well as its moral, political, and cultural standards. Female uniqueness and individuality were ignored and downplayed. As Mayfair Yang puts it, it was an era of gender erasure for women. [6] Femininity was subordinated into masculinity under a new guise, i.e., masculine collectivism. [7] Dai Jinhua calls this a "Hua Mulan" predicament: a woman becomes a legitimate hero by adopting the role of a man. [8]

The de-feminized women's images can be seen in official magazines and revolutionary posters from the 1960s and 1970s. Women were portrayed as socialist workers, army solders, and model farmers. Take one propaganda poster as an example: a woman wears an industrial work uniform against the background of a construction site with iron crane (Figure 1). What is highlighted is her social responsibility: she works along with men in the public.

FIGURE 1. "We are proud of participating in national Industrial construction," StefanLandsberger's Chinese Propaganda Poster Pages, available at http://www.iisg.nl/~landsberger/iron.html, and http://chineseposters.net.

Interestingly, despite Mao's attempt to re-construct women as tough and strong social citizens, beautiful female images were still employed for propaganda. Chen Xiaomei recounted that she was attracted by the voluptuous female bodies displayed in political posters during the Cultural Revolution.[9] As Foucault argued in *The History of Sexuality*, even in the darkest age when the sex was seemingly repressed, the discourses of sexuality actually prospered, in various disguises such as the medical (Foucault, 1978). Though the posters aimed at promoting the political agenda, the unusual embodiment of youth and elegance in the posters, such as "Changqing Points the Way," Chen argued, was another way to exploit the erotic.[10] The portrait of elegant female bodies in the politically correct visual arts, the posters, demonstrates an alternative representation of women under the guise of revolution.

The Changing Views on Femininity

Socioeconomic change in the post-Mao era gave rise to a series of social transformations, one of which was the politics of femininity. Four years after the Cultural Revolution, Zhang Xinxin published a short story, "Wo zai nali cuoguo le ni" (How did I miss you).[11]   Zhang uses the first-person voice in the main body of the novella and expresses her frustration over women's social responsibility and gender role. The protagonist "I," like other sent-down youths, spends her most precious years in the countryside, carrying heavy gunnysacks. She deliberately hunches her shoulders to conceal her feminine curves.   When she returns to the city, she becomes a bus conductor and also writes plays in her spare time out of her love for literature. In her day job, she deals with passengers and traffic. On the fully packed bus, she has to gather all her strength, using her arms, legs, hands, feet, and her whole body, and shove her way through the crowds.   She is one of many desperate people on the bus:

> If it hadn't been for the constant sound of that flat, monotonous tone all the conductresses used to call the names of the stops, which disguised her own pleasant, mellow voice, and for the shapeless blue cotton padded jacket with an artificial fur collar that she was wearing, it would have been hard to pick her out in that sea of blue and gray.[12]

At times when she tries with all her might and yet cannot move an inch in the crowd, and with most of the passengers watching her struggle with indifferent silence, she feels "a sudden rush of self-pity," and realizes she is a woman after all.[13]

Rough life turns the I-narrator into a tough woman. She is neither refined nor gentle. She has a hard time fitting in the social expectation of a woman with "virtue, yieldingness, forbearance, gentleness, quietness, reserve." [14] Instead, she quarrels with passengers and argues with her play director. She does not know how to express her love to the man she loves. She bitterly recalls:

> God, if there is one, made me a woman, but this society has demanded that I be like a man! So often I preferred to deliberately conceal my feminine traits just to survive, just to keep on going. [15]

When she realizes that she has lost the man she loves, she cannot help but question:

> You valued my struggle, but still required me to fit in with feminine standards. But if it hadn't been for my arrogant, masculine spirit, how would I have got to know you, how would we have trodden the same path? [16]

The problem raised in Zhang Xinxin's novella demystified the "iron woman" legacy: when a woman is as strong and capable as a man, does that mean she has realized gender equality? Once a woman has achieved so-called self-reliance and independence, how could she achieve a balance between her social obligations and the femininity that the society expects her to possess? Zhang's text reveals a woman's awkward situation: the success of her social role comes at the cost of sacrificing her femininity.

Zhang Xinxin was not alone in expressing her doubts. In the early 1990s, *Zhongguo funü* (Women of China), the official women's magazine, initiated a heated discussion on the issue of femininity. [17] It received many readers' letters; most of them acknowledging that physical appearance should play an important role in female identity. It was generally agreed that a woman should be beautiful for her self-esteem and sexual relationships, and a neatly dressed woman could symbolize the modernization of the nation in general. What was controversial was the question of to what extent women should beautify themselves: a moral issue circulated in *Women of China*. The approved though entirely subjective opinion in the magazine was that women should beautify themselves in a natural, graceful, healthy, and acceptable way consistent with good taste.

Though some readers did point out the hidden male-gaze behind beautiful femininity, the official acknowledgement, implied by the articles in *Zhongguo funü*, legitimized physical attractiveness and the public display of feminine traits such as beautiful clothes, hair styles, and makeup. Encouraged by ideological relaxation, commercial firms began to employ female images to promote various commodities. More and more attractive female images graced the magazine covers and public bulletin boards. Even *Zhongguo Funü* itself, caught between its role as the "throat and tongue" of the CCP and the immediate pressure to survive in a market economy, adopted the "double-cover" strategy to present different manifestations of femininity: properly dressed, realistic female professional figures on the front cover and sexually attractive female models selling commodities on the back cover.

On the front cover of *Zhongguo Funü* were real working people from different walks of life: model workers, athletes, and political leaders, epitomizing politically correct womanhood. Yet the back cover always provided an alternative femininity: attractive, young, and desirable. Take the Yue Sai (*Yuxi*) cosmetics ads as an example. Yue Sai's advertisements have occupied the back and inside covers of *Zhongguo Funü* longer than any other single company's during the mid and late 1990s. All of its commercial images involved young models, urban oriented and stylishly dressed. In one lipstick and nail polish advertisement, the dominant image is the face of a young Chinese girl with eye-catching red lips and fingernails. She holds a snow-white dog close to her face. Right above her head are a logo of the 1995 World Women's Conference, two English and Chinese captions that read "The Official Sponsor—1995 World Conference on Women," and a larger Chinese title of "Yue Sai Cosmetics." On the lower right corner of the page is the picture of the lipstick and nails. The caption says, "In Paris, when a fashionable woman goes out, she always holds her pet dog, and puts on her bright-colored lipstick: Yue Sai's Paris-pink (*bali fenhong*) lipstick and polish, forever new make-up!"[18]

The back cover image sheds light on a common way to represent attractive femininity in the new commercialization: the pleasant-looking image is related to both commodities and cultural imagination of the new lifestyle. The woman in the commercial is stylish, pretty, and associated with leisure and luxury, as suggested by the pet dog and her consumption of "Paris-pink" lipstick.[19] Who she is and what she does is not important. She is an anonymous symbol, identified by her globe-oriented make-up (Paris-pink) and middle-class lifestyle (pet dog). A new identity is implied: cosmopolitan, leisured, luxurious, and sexy.

Ostensibly, the commercial offers an escapist vision that is deceptively apolitical and totally different from the official ideology. However, the caption in the ad declaring the company as the "official sponsor" of 1995 Beijing World Conference on Women suggests that the commercial discourse negotiates and communicates with the mainstream politics. After all, it was to be a market economy "with Chinese characteristics."

The back cover image of *Zhongguo funü* was part of the booming commercial construction of attractive femininity. The consumers' market was flooded by fashion and cosmetic commodities. Various tips were offered on skin care and make-up strategies, which in turn created more consumption. Cosmetic surgery and the beauty pageant emerged, not only to bring the "best" femininity out of women, but also to introduce a transnational imagination. The fair skin and double eyelids, which are related to Caucasian femininity, were the common beauty ideals. The "Miss Asia" and "Miss World" competitions associated the local spectacle with global beauty consumption.

Who has been consuming the new beautiful femininity? Take car shows as an example. As the car was a luxurious consumer item and car shows a new popular showcase of wealth in big cities, there are always beautiful models posing beside the cars. Both objects were ideal parts of a successful man's life. The open display of commodities and femininity makes clear that the target audiences were men. Huang Shuqin puts it:

> Both the Cultural Revolution and commercialized society today are based on male power. In this respect, they are the same. The difference is that during the Cultural Revolution, men wanted women to become masculinized. In commercial society, however, men want women to become feminized. In both periods men are telling us what to do, so in terms of male power, they are basically equivalent.[20]

Her comments illuminate the role that patriarchal institutions have played in the construction of the feminine. As the beautiful feminine image was commercialized, it should come as no surprise that the images of female writers would also be highlighted, since previously high-toned cultural products, such as fiction and literary journals, which had hitherto been immune to such forces, had also become de facto commodities.

Born-in-the-70s Female Writers' Collective Debut: *Writer*

Seventies female writers made their collective debut in the July 1998 issue of *Writer* and immediately stunned the public with both their distinctive literary charm and striking physical appeal. Their debut was, it should be emphasized, both initiated and planned by three male intellectuals. In the winter of 1997, Zong Renfa, editor-in-chief of *Writer*; Shi Zhanjun, a literary critic and researcher at Shandong University; and Li Jingze, vice editor-in-chief of *Renming wenxue* (People's literature) had met in a hotel in the suburb of Beijing and had decided to bring forth a new literary voice and make it known to more readers.[21] The new voice was the "born-in-the-seventies female writers," who were in their twenties at that time. They chose *Writer* to launch a special issue on female writers.

Writer named the new voice "female writers born in the seventies" (*qishi niandai chusheng de nüzuojia zhuanhao*) and printed it as a trademark-like caption on the cover of the July issue of 1998. The issue collected the works of several high-profile female writers: Wei Hui, Mian Mian, Zhou Jieru, Wei Wei, Dai Lai, Jin Renshun, and Zhu Wenying. Other than presenting the writings of female writers, the journal also included writers' pictures, a self-introduction, male critics' comments, and the editors' notes. These components precede or follow the main bodies of the novellas, and make an interesting "paratext" that subtly invokes the gender power balance in representing the attractive femininity of women writers.[22]

Gérard Genette notes that the text is always accompanied by other elements such as the title, a preface, and illustrations, which surround and present the text, or "make it present." Genette calls this extra-literary production "paratext." The original French title of the book published in English as *Paratexts*, is *Seuils*, which means, literally, "thresholds." It describes a book's "vestibule," or border, which offers people "the possibility either of entering or of turning back." Genette summarizes several types of paratextual expression: the iconic (the illustration), the material (such as the typographical choices), or the purely factual (information about the work and its author). According to Genette, each element of the paratext has a position, related to the text itself. Although the "author" of the paratextual message is not necessarily the person who writes the text itself, paratext nevertheless comes to form part of the text. Both author and publisher are responsible both for the text and for the paratext. The paratext gives the information, and imparts an authorial or editorial intention or interpretation.[23]

With this theoretical framework, I would like to discuss the special issue in which these young female writers were presented. The front inside cover and back inside cover feature young writers' beautiful pictures. Inside the journal, each writer is an individual unit. Before and after the main texts are the visual and verbal paratexts: the writer's pictures, a few lines written by herself to introduce the pictures, the writer's own comments on her writing, and a male literary critic's overall evaluation of the writing style and the literary value.

At first sight what struck readers most was the visual representation of young women writers on the front and back inside covers, an image that offers a pertinent reading of the texts inside. The beautiful pictures serve as an opening for the reader. Without knowing a writer textually, readers meet her visually. This strategy of introducing writers resembles the promotion used for the entertainment star. Li Jingze, one of the three male initiators, however, denied the business intention behind this strategy. He said, "We had never met these writers before we decided to put them in one group and publish their novels. The so-called "beauty writers" were later promoted purely by the mass media." Yet he did admit that the plan to portray the women writers as a group was like a "conspiracy" (*mimou*), with the intention of creating a sensation.[24]

As if complementary to all the beautiful photos, the editor's comments on the back cover also pay special attention to these writers' fashionable femininity. It says, "The young writers are different from their predecessors. They are good-looking and beautiful. Like any modern women in the cosmopolitan cities, they are stylish in fashion and manner." The report affirms the writers' subversive influence on writing topics, subjectivities and styles. "They both shocked the senior editors and won good comments from younger readers." In a very positive tone, the report says the writers are new scenery in the literary field: "courageous," "brave," and "care-free."[25] Interestingly, the editor's comment is in the form of a news report, which suggests the newness and timeliness of the recent phenomenon. Though the report also points out certain weaknesses in the new-style writing, it confirms that female writers represent a new literary voice. They are projected as the new cultural imagination: smart urbanites and fashionable writers.

Each unit of an individual writer starts with the writer's three pictures and her own illustration of the pictures, followed by a male critic's introduction of the writer. The male critic introduces the writer, summarizes her writing style, and gives an "intellectual commentary." Right after the readers meet the writer visually, they encounter the male critic's judgment and evaluation of the female writer. It is with this (beautiful image plus intellectual commentary) framework that readers start to read the story, which follows. After the novel is the female writer's essay on her own writing philosophy, the last component of the unit.

Arranged in this way, the paratexts set up a framework in which the male intellectuals serve as the authority, the subject, and the viewer who observes and evaluates female writers. Male figures take the position of securely established literary predecessors and approvingly watch the rambunctious and brilliant newcomers. Most of the comments position the female writers in a culturally positive way, affirming the new energy these young writers have brought to the literary world.

Though it was male editors and critics who presented these writers to the public and judged them culturally and aesthetically, the female writers themselves were also involved in representing themselves for public scrutiny. Their active role in the making of "newly-new" generation stars and writers can been seen through their visual images in the pictures as well as their verbal texts.

Unlike Zhang Xinxin's writer protagonist, who even feels embarrassed by wearing a green scarf and attracting the stares of others, the women writers did not disguise their more or less narcissistic sense of their young and beautiful images. In stylish clothes and make-up, they pose like movie stars in the pictures they provided. The writer's brief explanation of the picture reveals her awareness of her good-looking appearance and the deliberate presentation of her femininity. Wei Hui, for example, is proud of herself as "a mainstream beauty."[26] Zhou Jieru explains one picture in which she looks up in her long hair, "Eighteen years old, I have a mature face."[27] For another picture in which she smiles in a fancy dress, she writes, "I learned to become womanly at twenty-one, yet people think I am artificial."[28] Zhu Wenying takes delight in the fact that people think she, in her short hair and melancholy expression, looks like Zhang Ailing, a famous woman writer from the 1930s. She names her picture "a picture for the deceased Zhang Ailing."[29]

All in all, these writers chose to present themselves as young, beautiful, and feminine. They subverted the writer's conventional serious, intellectual look. Their make-up, attire, expression, and posture deliver the message that they are physically attractive. Moreover, the well-groomed feminine beauty is associated with a new urban lifestyle. Mian Mian, for example, always holds a cigarette in her picture, a symbol of being "alternative" and cool. She tells us that she used to be a DJ in a club. Wei Hui does not disguise her zeal for night life. Her comments on a picture she took in a bar goes, "In the *Yinyang* bar, the decadent night life is about to begin. Yet I don't have time to dye my hair blue."[30] She says she "is trying hard to become a writer who really understands the modern romance and cool of the city."[31] The writers are proud of being the stylish and cool urbanites who could take advantage of the exciting city life.

Though fully enjoying being beautiful and materialistic, female writers also consciously relate themselves to their profession and craft a writing-related identity at the same time. Mian Mian supplies a picture in which she is a child standing in front of flowers. She writes, "I always made up stories for my doll in my childhood."[32] Wei Hui always mentions the fact that she is a Fudan University graduate. Dai Lai emphasizes that she often sits in her study and meditates "in the name of writing."[33] Wei Wei calls herself a "literary youth." Zhu Wenyi identifies with Zhang Ailing in both appearance and writing style.

In this way, the paratexts, jointly constructed by critics, editors, and the women writers, highlighted the attractive femininity as it is related to their literary production. By means of the pictures and brief comments, female writers presented themselves to the public as both unconventional female writers and cosmopolitan girls who love the new city excitement. The representations (the editor and critics' comments) and self-representation (the writers' own pictures and self-introductions) collaborated and presented female writes born in the seventies as a group of stars-cum-writers.

The glamorous beauty, however, was contained by subtle mechanisms exercised by the male editors. Though editors from both the capital, Beijing, and other provinces, Shangdong and Jilin, were involved in initiating the female writer showcase, it was eventually *Writer*, the provincial journal that became the stage for one of the major cultural shows in the late 1990s. I asked Li Jingze why they did not have *People's Literature* introduce the female writers. Li said, Beijing-based *People's Literature* is too mainstream. *Writer* was in a better position to present the women writers.[34] In this way, the female writers were strategically positioned in a geographically and culturally marginal, mediated space. Like the back cover image of *Women of China*, the presentation of the female writers carefully negotiated its confrontation with the political and literary mainstream.

It was not the first opportunity for those glam-lit writers to publish their novels. Yet this issue of *Writer* was a public space for the seventies female writers to make their collective debut. They struck a glamorous pose in the media and literary space. Their distinct treatment of their feminine bodies, both graphically and verbally, became a phenomenal yet controversial spectacle. Their collective performance won them the title of "beauty writer," a term that suggests highly visible femininity within the process of literary engagement.

The Prominence of Female Writers

As was expected, beautiful femininity was a big hit in the cultural market. It soon became a highly visible practice for the market to sell the images of female writers along with their works. Young women writers' beautiful pictures become part of the book content as well as a shrewd marketing strategy. For instance, the book cover image of *Shanghai Baby* is Wei Hui herself. Mian Mian's novella "La La La" and "Black Smoke" (Heiyan niaoniao) were published as pocket books along with fifty photos in April 1999.[35] Publishers realized a large profit and packaged "four beauty writers" (*si da meinü zuojia*): Yan Hong, Wang Tianxiang, Luo Yijia, and Tao Sixuan.[36] Over the Internet, "ten Internet beauty writers" were crowned as "beauty queens."[37] Moreover, the conception of "beauty" was linked with geographical locations. Most of the "beauties" were based in big cities such as Shanghai, Beijing and Guangzhou. Yet the "Shenzhen beauty writer" (Zhu Bi) and the "Changzhou beauty writer" (Zhou Jieru) also became relatively high-profile names. The whole scenario was like a beauty pageant. Beauties from different cities and locations competed with each other, not for a beauty title, but for sensation, readership and public attention.

In fact, selling writing and selling beautiful women was not a new phenomenon. As early as the 1930s, the book market in Shanghai already saw quite a few female writers' books and pictures. The famous writer Zhang Ailing (Eileen Chang) was noted for her unique writing and fancy dresses. *Xin nüxing* (New women), a 1933 left-wing movie, featured a publisher who wants to sell the female writer's beautiful picture along with her novel. These cases, though happening in different time periods, share the same profit-oriented marketing strategy. Women were employed and eroticized to attract attention from the public. In this sense, the 1990s moment can be seen as a revival of the 1930s' commercialization discourse, which was disrupted by the CCP's revolution and did not resume its momentum until the 1990s.

As glamour femininity turned out to be a popular literary plus, previous female writers were re-evaluated and re-addressed with their femininity as the focus. Zhang Ailing, for instance, was re-discovered and promoted as a *meinü* (beauty) rather than a *cainü* (literary woman) in the late 1990s.[38] Zhang's literary talent was downplayed, while her femininity was publicized as a highly visible object. Soon female writers stood out as the glamorous stars and dominated most of the "post-seventies" columns in various literary journals. For instance, in the 1999 issues of *Xiaoshuo jie*, there were only four males out of eleven writers. In *Shouhuo*, *Zhongshan* and *Changcheng*, there was only one male writer among the newly-new generation people who published novels between 1998 and 2000. Though writers born in the 1970s actually included a wide range of writers with different styles, it was the female writers who became the best known. Male writers were overshadowed. In both literary and commercial discourses, the general images of the post-seventies were projected as glamorous cosmopolitans.

Noting the increasing high profile of the female writers, critics, writers and literary journals began to claim that the female writers had "obscured" the writing of the seventies generation in general. Li Jingze, Zong Renfa and Shi Zhanjun met again and warned that the commercial promotion of the beauty writer hid the literary variety of her contemporaries. In their joint announcement, they claimed that businessmen had glamorized writers into stars and sold a whole fantasy of a new urban lifestyle, which in turn made female writers of this kind appear especially commercially attractive. The "star-ized" stylish writing overshadowed not only male writers in general, but also other women writers with different writing styles.[39]

In April 1999, *Furong* (Hibiscus) published another special issue on "reshaping the post-seventies generation," which aimed at bringing to light the varieties of writing styles developed by writers born in the 70s. Chen Wei, who initiated the term "seventies generation," used the pen name Li An to rebuke both female writers and journal editors. According to him, female writers, like any writers of "stylish female writing" in popular chic magazines use the name of writing in hope of getting attention and obtaining fame and wealth. Ill-intentioned journal editors, he claimed, also focused more on the sensation rather than literary value, enabling the "stylish women writers" to overshadow the literary varieties of the post-seventies generation. Chen therefore proposes the real literary and aesthetic re-construction of the seventies:

We hope Chinese literature can achieve real independence on a higher level. We hope Chinese literature can break away from the domination of politics, social didacticism, religion, culture, utilitarianism, and fashion, and return to the construction of its own subjectivity. Meanwhile, we do not resist ideological, moral and intellectual literature. But we do think that literariness and artistry should be the primary characteristic of literature, which for a long time did not get good attention from writers and the whole literary circle.[40]

Chen Wei's comment originated out of his concern for literature itself. Yet the beauty writer phenomenon extended well beyond the literary arena. It was related to the social imagination at a time when catching the new trend of globalization and consumption was floating in the air, a point that I will elucidate in the following chapters. As demonstrated by the special issue of *Writer*, beautiful images suggested a new urban style. As both the subject and the object of new desire, the beauty writer not only articulated women's fantasies, but also embodied men's hidden desires. The fact that a woman could actively articulate and actualize the desire in a direct way certainly put men on the defensive. It was her social symbolic meaning, along with their literary presentation, that brought her into the public spotlight. That is why Chen Wei's call for pure, artistic literary style did not achieve his original goal of reshaping the 70s generation. Instead, female writers continued to flourish and outshine male writers as an alternative in both the literary arena and the commercial market. In the following chapters, I will critically analyze the "beauty myth:" what specific cultural symbols female writers created and how this imagination was tied to collective desire at the moment of social transformation.

CHAPTER TWO

The Changing Faces of Ephemeral Youth: A Reading of Mian Mian

Beauty writers, or glam-lit writers, belong to the group of seventies writers, a casual category that differentiated the works of the newly-new generation from earlier literary styles. It is not uncommon for Chinese literary critics to group writers based on the distinctive characteristics of their writings. Earlier literary movements or schools, such as "scar literature," "root searching" or "avant-garde," were named because their literary products share common motifs. Scar literature is given this name because it exposes the trauma brought about by the Cultural Revolution. Root-searching writers focus on seeking cultural roots in remote countryside and among marginal people. Avant-garde writers group those who experiment with new modes of expression and unfamiliar writing techniques. The "Seventies" category was uncommon in that the writers so labeled were grouped according to their age. By boldly or casually categorizing writers as an elastic group of "writers born in the seventies," critics shifted their attention to the issue of *time*. On the one hand, the time is constructed as it is related to the broad effects of a particular era on a generation of individuals. On the other hand, the time also implies the *timeliness* and *time-sensitiveness*. The newly-new generation would not be this sensational were it not for its timely appearance at the turn of the new century. In fact, the playful naming of beauty writers also sheds lights on the heyday of youth, the prime of physical attractiveness, as "beauty" itself is also time-sensitive and fashion-oriented.

The 1990s marked a new phase of cultural development, and seventies writers came into their twenties at that time. They emerged in the literary arena and the mass media as a group of *linglei* young people, unconventional and cool. They constructed youthfulness with multiple focuses in the texts as well as in real life. In this chapter, I will read the fictional narrative of "cruel youth" and the youth subculture, represented by Mian Mian and her novel *Candy* (Tang).[1]

Candy was categorized as a "youth novel" (*qingchun xiaoshuo*) by a Taiwan online bookstore, along with Wang Meng's *Qingchun wansui* (Long live youth), Wang Shuo's *Dongwu xiongmeng* (Animal ferocity) and Han Han's *San cong men* (The third way).[2] The cruel youth in Mian Mian's novels expressed two major problems: youth and illness. In growing up with growing pains is also the recovery of the physical and psychological ailments. Drawing inspiration from her own experience, in *Candy* as well as her many other earlier writings, Mian Mian expressed uneasiness and an intensified awareness of youth as a problem in a metropolitan China undergoing the process of globalization. Marginal youths in the early stage of the reform era, as represented by Mian Mian, stood out as the willful counterculture youngsters who passively resisted the dominant culture. Yet it was through their subculture resistance that they attracted attention from the mainstream and eventually achieved their own cultural niche in it. On the one hand, the mainstream, by means of commercialization, appropriated the subculture rebellion, sold it as cool and thereby created an alternative imaginary. On the other hand, the marginal youths, as they grew up and matured, consciously chose to cooperate with the mainstream and eventually fulfilled the imagination of the urban middle class, and therefore drifted away from their initial rebellious position.

Youth in Historical Retrospective

Youth and youthfulness are recurring themes in modern Chinese literary discourse. At the beginning of the 20th century, iconoclastic youth was constructed as a symbol of hope and the future in the social transformation. *Xin qingnian* (New Youth), a magazine founded by Chen Duxiu in 1915, is a good example. Targeting young people, the magazine expressed a political agenda of anti-imperialism and anti-feudalism. In 1916, Li Dazhao wrote an essay titled "Qingchun" (Spring) to eulogize youth. Spring implies awakening and new life, and Li believed that young people have a spring-like quality. He enthusiastically wrote, "With their Spring ego, they will create Spring families, Spring countries and nations, a Spring humanity, Spring earth and a Spring universe, enriching an unlimited life with happiness."[3] Li employed the image of spring to pay tribute to young people whose youthfulness, energy and courage could make a difference. Youth represented a new social force that could bring change to China, which suffered under the political turmoil brought by internal social erosion and foreign imperialism.

Though there were also literary images of confused, disoriented, and decadent youths, such as Yu Dafu's displaced young student who suffers from hypochondria ("Sinking"), Ding Ling's willful modern girl ("Miss Sophia's Diary"), Lu Yin's girl student with heart disease ("Someone's Tragedy") and Zhang Ailing's many indifferent, self-focused young women, the pale, sick and disoriented young protagonists were soon invigorated by revolutionary passion. As Tang Xiaobing argues, the death of the last Tubercular in *Cold Night* epitomizes the end of the antihero characters, and the sick body was removed from the literary discourse and was replaced by energetic, romantic young people who wholeheartedly dedicate themselves to the glorious moment of saving the nation and establishing a new society.[4]

In *Qingchun wansui* (Long live youth), Wang Meng portrayed a group of young high school (girl) students, who passionately devote themselves to the heroic construction of a new socialist China in the 1950s. The title, "Long Live Youth," itself reveals a romantic ideal that youth can be perpetual. In the novel, the young protagonists denounce the old feudalist families and embrace the newly founded China. They study diligently and help each other adjust to the new nation. They cheer for the victory of the socialist regime and celebrate the age of idealism and innocence. The novel ends with young students celebrating their graduation from high school at Tian'anmen square. They gather in front of Chairman Mao's portrait, hold back tears of emotion and solemnly swear, "We will do a good job!"[5] While they sing songs and walk back from the Tian'anmen square, the golden sunshine of the morning is illuminating the top of the Monument of the People's Hero.

The morning sun metaphor was employed by Mao Zedong to eulogize the vigorous youth of the new generation. The utopian portrayal of the youth in Wang Meng's novel reflects the cultural status of youth in socialist China. Youth symbolized a young nation, a bright future and a romantic ideal. The collective optimism reflects an age of euphoric passion, utopian fantasy, and poetic expectation as the new socialist regime provided a glorious dream and a new imagination for its people.

The utopian passion gave way to a more rational intellectual reflection on reality and a pragmatic approach toward developing the economy in the 1980s and 1990s. The grand narrative of the morning-sun youth was ruptured and deconstructed by a very different discursive narration of youthfulness. The anarchistic young "hooligans" and angry young folk (*fenqin*) soon filled up the ideological vacuum created by the economical and political transformation. Wang Shuo wrote a series about playful urban youngsters who ridicule the establishment in novels such as *Wan zhu* (Master of mischief), *Qianwan bie ba wo dang ren* (Please don't call me human) and *Wan de jiushi xintiao* (Playing for thrills). Film director Zhang Yuan depicted indifferent, decadent youth who seek salvation through rock'n'roll in *Beijing zazhong* (Beijing bastards), with rock'n'roll "godfather" Cui Jian as the main actor. These young people in the burgeoning market economy maintain a cynical, indifferent detachment from the mainstream and indulge themselves in the newly found individualistic life-styles.

Mian Mian, like many of her predecessors, wrote on the subject of youth. Her focus was the underground world and the pain, frustration, fear, and loneliness felt by struggling marginal youngsters. As Mian Mian claimed, she was probably the first to publish a novel on drugs in China.[6] Mian Mian portrayed youth as plagued by sickness and self-destructive tendencies. Hers is the time of cruel youth, the darkest growing phase. Not only did Mian Mian return to youth problems and illness, she also put medical and clinical discourses back into writing. Both trends were discussed and practiced by the May Fourth writers at the beginning of the twentieth century. Yet the *fin de siècle* debauched youth and the clinical function of writing are drastically different from the May Fourth projects. Both desperate youth and salvation-oriented writing are self-absorbed, related to the individual experience of growing up in the transitional era of the nineties.

Youth Born in the Seventies

Writers born in the seventies grew up in the transitional period from the socialist ideology to the globally oriented market economy. They witnessed and experienced the social and cultural changes from the seventies to the nineties. They barely had any memory of the traumatic experiences, poverty, and hardship suffered by earlier generations. Zhu Wenying, one of the seventies writers, says, "Compared with the previous generation, the real, collective 'big events' were absent in our life when we grew up... The so-called 'wounded experience,' if there were any, was also individual, fragmented... We don't have a collective passion like our predecessors do."[7] They spent their childhood or early adolescence in the 1980s and though they were educated at school to follow socialist teachings, they were also exposed to various new ideas, practices, and commodities brought by rapid economic growth. They were the earliest group of people to listen to pop songs and drink Coca Cola. Caught in the tension between the formal socialist education and the dazzling changing reality, they nevertheless enjoyed new opportunities. "We are the beneficiaries of economic growth. I do not think most of us have known real hardship like those born in the sixties." admitted Zhou Jieru in an interview.[8]

Though China of the 1990s is a central reference point for the majority of the young female writers, readers of their novels can hardly see the nineties as a grand historical moment. Instead, what we read are the fragments and pastiche of a changing lifestyle: the motion-charged space such as bars, restaurants, nightclubs, fashion stores, shopping centers, and hotels; the new lifestyles like partying, dating, and clubbing, and the restless urban young people and their anxiety, frustration and confusion. As Wu Liang suggests, here history is replaced by the "historical mood;" the mood at a particular historical moment and bought by the changing society.[9] The historical reality is therefore highly subjective and individualized, with writers' "selves," individual sentiments, and memories as the focus.

Their self-absorbed writing style has been subjected to much criticism. Ge Hongbing, one of the earliest critics to pay attention to the newly-new generation, for example, criticizes it at the very beginning: "Literature should be engaged in a kind of comprehensiveness, not just in the compilation of details," and "it should take a broad view and therefore reflect a grand time."[10] He suggests that the novels of the new people, though creating new aesthetics, lacked the classic elements of literature. Though Ge Hongbing challenges the "grand-narrative" mentality on many occasions, his view is still built upon the assumption that the standard or classic literature should have "grandness" in focus. Ge believed that the novels of the new generation were too concerned with triviality, the self and the subjective feeling and were therefore too narrow.

As if to respond to Ge's comments, Wei Wei defends herself this way, "I like 'small' men. By instinct, I am repelled by heroes. I like ordinariness, and I am scared by the epic."[11] According to Wei Wei, ordinary people do not have many chances to experience the thrilling events. Their life is saturated by ordinary, mechanical routines. It is the very "small" part of life that fascinates her. Wei Wei said, "I am the one who lacks social responsibility. I don't devote myself in the hectic wave of our time... I don't know what young people are thinking about...I have no feeling about our era (*shidai*)."[12] Wei Wei's words indicate a general trend in the literary writing: writers tend to understand the grand age through their personal perspective.

Zhu Wenying claims there is no clear-cut line between the "small stories" and "big events." "Big events" might be embodied through trivial daily life since the grand background is always there, as an overarching background that influences people's writing.[13] From this angle, the representation of personal life is also an alternative way to narrate a large history. Though direct reference to the hectic and energetic 1990s is generally absent in the novels, the grandness of history is privatized, trivialized, and minimized, embodied through the narration of the individual experience which, to a large extent, is the young writers' growing pains, their searching for identity and for a sense of belonging. For instance, Zhou Jieru writes on her rebellious teenage years ("Recalling the age of being a problem girl," *Huiyi zuo yige wenti shaoniü de shidai*), and Wei Wei seeks her destiny by journeying from city to city ("Starting from Nanjing," *Cong Nanjing chufa*). Wei Hui's interest in a girl's growing sexual consciousness could be seen in novels such as "Ai Xia" and "Pistol of desire" (*Yuwang shouqiang*).

Among them, Mian Mian's youthful experience is the darkest, related to adventures in the underground world of crime, drugs and sex, and her narration is the most fragmented, symbolizing the fragmented memory of a highly subjective experience. The fragmented narrative of self-destructive youth is best embodied in *Candy*. Composed of several stories, such as "One Patient," "Acid Lover" and "We are scared," which Mian Mian wrote between 1994 and 1999, *Candy* does not have a coherent storyline. It is a combination of many individually written pieces. Nevertheless, various writing segments conjure up the life experience of the protagonist and other marginal youths who emerge in the new reality of the market economy. Besides the format, Mian Mian's narrative language is also short and terse, full of rock'n'roll rhythm.[14] For instance, Mian Mian described the mood of her protagonist this way:

> The moon is my sun; its rays penetrate my room, making me realize how depressed I am. When I lay my body down, I can hear the sound of my blood flowing. It is a feeling that is both inspiring and oppressive. So many tedious efforts, my body is cold and frail... To hell with language! To hell with orgasms! To hell with whores! To hell with love! My body and I just want to throw up! If there ever comes a day when I can have an orgasm without having to depend on a man, I will lie down in front of the moon and have a good cry.[15]

The tension between lines represents instability, restlessness, and desperation.

Candy was first published in a prestigious literary journal *Shouhuo* and also printed as a book by Zhongguo xiju chubanshe. It quickly became a best-seller. Yet soon, the book was taken off the market by the authorities due to its portrayal of the tabooed dark subjects, its exposition of the *linglei* community, and its rejection of the mainstream. The banning of the novel turned the author into a young rebel who has the courage to pinch a political nerve. Because of the political interpretation of the book, *Candy* was translated into English, French, Japanese, and Spanish, and helped Mian Mian achieve international success. Interestingly, Mian Mian's mainstream triumph changed her from a willful, wild young patient to a cool public eclectic. The making of *Candy*, as well as the consequent fate of *Candy*, is the manifestation of the transformation of a marginal youth into a popular celebrity.

The Paradoxical Faces of Youth in the Transnational Condition

Mian Mian claims, "Some people relate youth to happiness. I relate youth to being out of control. Mine is the cruel youth."[16] Mian Mian's pessimistic view derives from her own life experience. Mian Mian's real name is Wang Shen, and she was born in 1970 in Shanghai. She dropped out of high school at the age of seventeen and started to write and publish novels when she was a teenager. Her earliest novels are mostly on cruel youth, the dark adventure of marginal young urban dwellers. Characters in Mian Mian's novels include drifters, unsuccessful musicians, unemployed youngsters, drug-addicts, prostitutes, punks, slackers, homosexuals, artists, and various people who are desperately struggling in the cities. Disoriented and confused, these young characters are the rootless group in the metropolises.

Narrated mostly in the first person, *Candy* centers on the experience and feeling of a woman named Hong. The novel relates the protagonist's life from indulgence in drugs, alcohol, and hopeless relationships to salvation in writing. Hong, the mirror image, to some degree a self-portrait, of the writer herself, is a problem girl. She quits school, runs away from home, joins a band and wanders about in different cities. She feels trapped in her dysfunctional relationships with men and seeks sanctuary in drugs and alcohol. In her physical and psychological depression, writing saves her from destruction. By recounting Hong's turbulent youth, Mian Mian constructs youth in *Candy* as disoriented, hopeless, desperate, paranoid, and decadent.

As a rebellious youngster, Hong maintains a paradoxical relation with the mainstream. On the one hand, she rejects elitism, intellectuals, and the middle class. On the other hand, she relies on her parents' generation for financial and emotional support. She is not strong enough to completely break away from the mainstream institutions, nor does she intend to do so. Because of this, her resistance is more of a self-absorbed mood, sentiment, and temperament than any real action.

Born into a well-off intellectual family, Hong refuses, as a child, to study the oil painting *Mona Lisa* and listen to the classical music in which her father tries to cultivate her interest. Both the oil painting and the classical music symbolize elite and intellectual taste. By saying no to both, Hong rejects high culture as well as the authority of a father figure. She later denounces both family and society by quitting school and joining a wandering band. She chooses to exile herself from the adult space, home, and school, to the marginal, flowing spaces. She drifts from city to city and wanders in Xinjiang, Shenzhen and Beijing. The places that she frequents are bars, clubs, rented apartments and hotels, the newly emerged unstable spaces with minimum control by authorities. She becomes one of the many rootless people such as Little Shanghai and Little Xi'an, whose names imply a sense of displacement. They abandon their hometowns in hopes of seeking fortune and luck in big cities such as Shenzhen, the Special Economic Zone that first opened to the outside. They enter the city as outsiders and soon sink into deeper despair.

Hong not only spatially exiles herself; she also escapes into the sanctuary of the night. The day time, which implies the "normal" engagement of career and life, is not her favorite time. Night, associated with escapism, gives her a sense of belonging. She takes night as her "lover" and "sweetheart."[17] In fact, Mian Mian herself, as a party and music promoter, is especially infatuated with the night. Her fascination with the darkness can be seen from her other novel titles such as "Yige jiaorou zaozuo de wanshang" (A deliberate night) and "Ni de heiye, wo de baitian" (Your night, my day). Mian Mian even compares her own writing to "a bottle breaking at midnight," sharp and nerve racking.[18] The night provides alternative time for an alternative urban lifestyle. By turning to the dark night for pleasure, indulgence and excitement, Mian Mian rejects and subverts the morning-sun metaphor formerly so meaningful for young people. Her attachment to the nighttime conforms to her choice of being an alternative urbanite in reality.

Hong has to choose this lifestyle since she and her friends do not know how to join the majority. She explains it this way,

> We weren't interested in other people's lives, we were sensitive and self-doubting, we didn't believe what we read in the newspaper, we were afraid of failure, and yet the thought of resisting some temptation made us anxious. We wanted to be on stage, to be artists. We kept on spending other people's money, dreading the day when all of this would change. We didn't want to become good little members of society, nor did we know how. Anyway, we would tell ourselves, we're still young.[19]

This paragraph betrays the anxiety of the marginal youngsters like Hong. They refuse to identify with the mainstream and behave as a counterculture minority. Yet they also aspire to be at the center of attention. The paradox turns their initial rebellion into an attempt to get the potential recognition from the adult, with "being young" as a convenient excuse for their self-indulgence.

Therefore, though Hong denounces her parents' generation, as well as the mainstream, she still mentally and financially relies on her parents. Hong's father gives her money and sends her to the clinic when she is physically and psychologically sick. Saining, one of the male protagonists, lives on money from his mother, who works in Japan. The parent-figures play the role of saviors. As Hong says, "I am naturally sensitive, but am not intelligent. I am a natural rebel, but I am not strong. I think that is my problem." [20] Hong's defiance of and reliance on her father is an allegory of her generation, whose resistance to the established figures is more of a ritual and a performance than a real breaking away from the majority.

There are several male characters in the novel, Saining, Kiwi, Apple, Tan Tan and Bug. Hong maintains an on-and-off relationship with Saining. She discovers that he cheats on her. Their life becomes a mess when he becomes addicted to heroin and she to alcohol. They become destructive and violent, as she cuts her veins and he cracks his head. They feel desperate and helpless since they cannot pull themselves out of their trouble. The second group of male characters are Kiwi and Apple, Hong's middle school classmates. Hong, Kiwi and Apple keep a strange triangle relationship between friendship and love. Their stories are intertwined with Hong's recalling of her middle school trouble, her awareness of the rapidly changing reality of Shanghai, and the homosexual friends she has. Hong at this time pulls herself out of her drug problem and turns to writing as therapy. After that, Hong begins to date Tan Tan, a violent, abusive man. Tan Tan soon dies a mysterious death. Hong is suspected as the murderer and is questioned by the police.[21] Towards the very end of the story, a man named Bug comes into Hong's life and reminds her of the panic of AIDS.

Interestingly, most of the men with whom Hong associates have something to do with the transnational imaginary. Born in China, Saining holds a British passport. His "non-Chinese" and "non-West" personality isolates him from people around him. Working as a stylist, one of the newest professions in China's metropolis, Kiwi flies back and forth between Shanghai and America. Bug comes back from New York. Meanwhile, their transnational experiences also correlate with various aspects of the subculture: rock'n'roll, disease, loose sex and drugs, which subtly suggests the global subculture condition as it is presented in the local context. The young urban female connects with the globe-hopping males and joins in the popular youth image of clubs, music, drugs and travel.

These portrayals are closely related to China's opening up to the global circulated ideologies, though the author does not directly confront this grand age. At some point, the protagonist blames her and her fellows' delinquency on the new urban condition that is the result of economic development. It is in Shenzhen, the border town, the first Special Economic Zone, where she sinks to the bottom. When her father brings her back to her hometown Shanghai, Hong curses Shenzhen this way, "I swore I would never come back to this town in the south ever again. This weird, plastic, bullshit Special Economic Zone, with all the pain and sadness, and the face of love, and the whole totally fucked-up world of heroin, and the late-1980s gold rush mentality, and all that pop music from Taiwan and Hong Kong."[22] Though contact with outside influences brings new energy and lifestyle to the urban culture, it also lures the young protagonists to the euphoric illusion of drugs and alcohol and the promise of euphoria.

36

Illness and Youth

Mian Mian claims in many of her fictional pieces that she is "a patient," "dependent on drugs," and a "nightmare" for her parents.[23] Even after she recovered from drug addiction, she constantly struggled with depression.[24] In *Candy*, the protagonist suffers from all sorts of physical and mental sicknesses: asthma, overdoses, alcoholism, hypochondria, and hysteria. Tortured by the illnesses, she loses her voice, appetite, hair, and health. Besides the physical deformity, she is caught in deep psychological despair. She becomes weak, hypersensitive and melancholic. From her pathologic perspective, she is surprised to discover that the world she knows is full of patients and sufferings. People around her are hopelessly addicted to drugs and alcohol and constantly grasped by the panic of rotten bodies and death. The nervous, paranoid, disoriented, desperate marginal youth is total subversion of the energetic, hopeful, and confident youth that had been promoted during the socialist decades.

In both *Illness as Metaphor* and *AIDS and Its Metaphors*, Susan Sontag urged an anti-metaphorical reading of diseases.[25] Yet it is hard not to read illness as a metaphor in the modern Chinese literary discourse, which started from a patient, the madman depicted by Lu Xun. Illness has been frequently employed as a metaphor by modern Chinese writers, who use it to satirize social and individual problems. The hypochondriac youth portrayed by Yu Dafu and the tubercular by Ba Jin, for instance, reflect personal anguish over the national crisis, as well as helplessness. The imagery of physical deformity in Mian Mian's text is also related to the new age. As the protagonist searches for an alternative identity, she sinks into a self-indulgence brought on by the ideological vacuum.

In the I-narrator's physical and psychological crisis, it is her father who brings her home and sends her to a rehab clinic. Upon her arrival at the hospital, she discovers that everybody wears the same clothes. Then her eccentric nurse's aide, who is also a psychiatric patient and a murderer herself, tells her that she is being housed with the mental patients. In the painful process of medication, she realizes the power of authority: "I thought that the Communist Party (and that included my father) was pretty intense, putting drug addicts who were trying to clean up in here along with homicidal maniacs so that we should all be cured together."[26] The hospital, where the adult regulation is imposed, becomes a symbol of power. Authority, in the forms of the father figure and the rehab clinic, "normalizes" her.

Eventually, it is writing that saves the I-narrator from utter despair. "Writing came to me on the doctor's orders."[27] For her, "writing is a method of transforming corruption and decay into something wonderful and miraculous."[28] Similar to Lu Xun's conception of literature as a medicinal discourse, Mian Mian takes writing as a remedy. Unlike Lu Xun's goal of saving the nation and children, Mian Mian writes for self-salvation. Lu Xun writes as a doctor, and Mian Mian as a patient. Mian Mian's subculture experience ironically parallels the mainstream narration. As Mian Mian says, "Really I was writing simply to understand myself, for my good friends, and sometimes for the men to whom I'd once been close."[29]

Mian Mian writes for self-salvation and Lu Xun not, but the issue is no longer merely a matter of motivation as if the author could domesticate the tool of language like a house pet. Rather, a more interesting issue appears on the horizon — what relationship to language has Mian Mian forged in this postmodern/modern urban sphere that would make language a tool of healing that nonetheless resists the normalizing power inherent in institutions with power over the body. In the same way, Foucault suggests that the fact of sexual expression shifts the possibilities and expectations for language.[30] Mian Mian's use of writing for recovery and survival is not merely a tool for psychoanalytic healing, but recognition that self-expression through language transforms her in relation to the alienating conditions of modern life. For Mian Mian, writing serves not merely to describe the darkness of the clinic but to transform, to call forth light to illuminate a space for expression and redescription, whose absence would otherwise leave her merely subject to the normalizing forces at play in the institution.

Both the illness and recovery can be read as the social metaphors for the problem of plagued youth, the becoming of Mian Mian's generation in the new urban context. Later, Mian Mian becomes a mother. Meanwhile, her father is diagnosed with cancer. As the old adult is becoming physically weak and waning, the new adult is coming into being. Both made Mian Mian more "rational" and "reasonable" than before.   In her new book *Xiongmao* (Panda sex), she told readers that they are going to be disappointed if they expect to see "sex, lust, drugs, my complaint... and suicide," because "I do not have this inside me anymore."[31]

Mian Mian believes that she is different from other writers born in the seventies: "They are within the institution. They have jobs. They went to colleges. They want to join the Writers' Association. I belong to street culture."[32] She emphasizes that her writing is from her own real pain, and she discloses the real self-destructive impulse and darkest youthful experience. Therefore she hates the fact that her pain has been interpreted as being cool and that she is categorized in the beauty writers group. She regards the term "beauty writers" as a sign of a seriously sick society, "Our time is ill, seriously ill. Writers are ill. Medias are ill. Critics are ill. Readers are ill."[33] The society is sick because it disrespects female writers. The illness of critics and readers is their voyeuristic reading of female writers' self-representation. The problem of female writers is their "morbid" (*bingtai*) self-obsession. The media even called on scholars to "feel the pulse" (*haomai*) of beauty writers, a traditional Chinese medical term metaphorically used to diagnose writers' problems.[34] Wei Hui, for instance, was criticized as being *wubing shenyin*, that is, making a fuss about an imaginary illness, or moaning without being sick. Because her story was fabricated, she was accused of not being sincere and honest, of using the pain as a superficial code and ignoring its real meaning.[35]

The Changing Faces of Mian Mian

It is true that Wei Hui herself was never addicted to drugs. If it was superficial for her to speak for the drug addicts, Wei Hui was certainly not alone in appropriating pain as part of the style of the urban cool. Much to Mian Mian's chagrin, her drug addiction, her pain, has been commercially packaged and became a cool commodity. The "cruel" has been sold as the "cool."[36] Mian Mian strongly condemned the media that misrepresented her image. She accused the media of delivering the message: "I am cool! Because I take drugs! I am cool, because I have loose sex!" She thought it ridiculous that the serious problems became entertaining tabloid news.[37] She was angry at the cover image of *Candy* designed by a Taiwan publishing house, for it sells the novel as a cheesy love story in the Taiwan market. She even suggested readers tear off the cover before they read the novel.[38]

Angela McRobbie suggests that the youth culture can be commercially appropriated, yet young people continue to reinterpret those forms and invent new meanings for it again.[39] Though Mian Mian's suffering was appropriated as a lucrative commodity, she nevertheless took advantage of the publicity and created her own niche in mainstream culture. It is through her subculture experience that she puts herself at the center of the media and literary attention and achieved transnational success. Though she openly denounced the mainstream institutions initially, she was also pleased to have her talents recognized by the majority.

Mian Mian was not completely uninvolved in selling and cashing in on her cruel youth as cool. Her ambition of reaching a wider readership is already seen in *Candy*. Though initially writing for self-healing, "(a)s I wrote, I became more ambitious, and I wanted lots of people to read what I wrote—I wanted the whole world to see what I'd written."[40] In fact, she was the first author sponsored by a business group.[41] In 1999, she accepted the sponsorship of "Jazz Rum Sparkling." The company bought five hundred copies of *La La La*, which was later included as one chapter of *Candy*, and gave them to readers. Before *Candy* was officially published, Mian Mian organized a party named "Candy" and toured twenty cities in China. The goal was to publicize "party culture," "rock'n'roll culture" and "dancing music culture."[42] These events turned Mian Mian's underground experience into a glamorous show. With the incorporation of transnational capital, her subculture adventure was romanticized into a new urban imagery of partying and clubbing. Mian Mian was certainly very active in capitalizing on her passionate and chaotic youthful experiences. She adapted to the new cultural and social opportunities and stood out as a representative of the urban alternative, a pop figure in the public.

After Mian Mian married and became a mother, a rebellious daughter grew into a caring parent. Her essays started to express the maternal love she feels when she is watching the sweet face of her daughter and her desire to become a good adult. One essay was written as an affectionate monologue with her daughter, "You learn to walk, and mommy learns to be a mommy... We grow up together."[43] The newspaper also reported how Mian Mian decorated the new apartment she bought after she divorced. The essay, titled "Mian Mian lives in the name of partying," detailed Mian Mian's unique tastes in her own family space: "Mian Mian only has two requirements: the living room should be big enough to hold parties for many people. It should also be cozy enough for her to quietly admire the Huangpu River when she is alone."[44] The "home" signals Mian Mian's change from an anarchistic, self-indulgent young woman to an eclectic: she returned home, though she also brought the party to her living room. The drifting girl finally settles down and secures her own space in the bustling city.

Meanwhile, Mian Mian also wrote columns on emotions and relationships for popular magazines. Right after the ban on her books was removed, Mian Mian published an essay collection, *Shejiao wu* (Social dance). The title itself implies Mian Mian's changing attitude toward her relation with her surroundings, a sharp contrast to the paranoid protagonists in *Candy* who did not know how to interact with the society.[45] Finally, Mian Mian started to "socialize." The book is composed of short essays on relationships, love, friendship, and mental health. Essays in the collection produced the image of a globe-traveling woman with a stylish Shanghai life with many dazzling parties. The essays, such as "A weekend in London," "Melancholy in a motel at Milan airport," and "Shanghai girls like Latin music," imply a globally mobile, middle-class lifestyle: it is the newly established reality of Mian Mian. In an essay titled "The last rose of summer," Mian Mian relates her globe-hopping life: promoting her book in Italy, visiting her daughter in Britain, and going to Paris.[46] The romantic configuration of life on the global road is drastically different from her previous portrayal of darkness, pain and desperation. Mian Mian metamorphosed from a girl on the bumpy road of China to a glamorous woman trotting on the global highway.

Mian Mian's cooperation with the commercial and popular discourses makes her a high-profile figure in the urban mainstream, which further publicizes her earlier subculture experience. She started to serve as a "spokeswoman" for Chinese subculture youth in international forums. As the only representative from Asian countries, she participated in the seminar of Club Health 2002 organized by World Health Organization and some organizations in Italy. In the seminar, she discussed issues such as "safe dancing," "safe club night life," "safe sex" and so on.[47] Meanwhile, Mian Mian also played a role of a "savior" for the struggling marginal youth. She condemned the harmful effects of drugs on people, organized a charity concert to save street kids and sought to help people who suffer depression. By now, Mian Mian has become an international promoter of the rational lifestyle. She legitimized her originally marginal way of life while conforming to mainstream life.

As Mian Mian recovered from her illness and grew into an adult, her public image changed from the initial problem girl to a cool young urbanite, a sophisticated cosmopolitan woman, and a globally mobile spokeswoman for marginal youth. The paradoxical realtion between the rebellious youngsters and the mainstream can also be seen in many other cases. Chun Shu, another younger rebel, for instance, aspired to be admitted by Beijing University or Harvard University.[48] The changing image of Mian Mian implies the growing up of a young generation.

The time is constructed in Mian Mian's novels as the willful youth and eclectic grownup, both of which were packaged as a cool urban adventure in a cosmopolitan space. In the next chapter, I will focus on the issue of space associated with young female writers, who thrived in the postmodern clash of cyber and urban spaces. As the most energetic social group in the 1990s, young writers always were caught up with the most up-to-date media and technology and therefore extended their literary space from the real to the virtual.

CHAPTER THREE

Cyber Writing as Urban Fashion

This chapter focuses on the *double space* where seventies writers carried out their literary engagement. The space of female writers and their writing unfolded on two stages: the real and the virtual. The real existed in the writers' ties with the city, the metropolis, and various urban settings. The virtual was realized on the Internet, the newly emergent technology-enabled cyberspace of the late 1990s. The interplay of the real and the virtual enlarged the literary space available to these young writers, and, at the same time, turned them into a stylish urban class who integrated the most up-to-date media into their lives and careers. The emergence and the involvement of cyberspace in the fictional narrative expanded the imagination of the urbanites. Urban-based cyberspace provided a way to imagine the other, an alternative, carefree community where people could break away from the restrictions of real life, and get access to what is inaccessible in reality. To some extent, this ability did empower people in real urban space, as they gained access to an extra/alternative space to voice their opinions and act out their ideas. Yet when people hid themselves behind cyber names and infatuated themselves with cyberspace communication, their interaction with real-life surroundings was reduced. After all, cyberspace cannot be separated from real life. When the initial rosy imagination of cyberspace as an other was gone, they eventually put their feet back down on the earth and return to their real roots, i.e., the urban reality.

At the turn of the century, not everybody in China had access to the Internet. Cyberspace was only available for a relatively small percentage of financially or culturally privileged urbanites. Urban-cyber space was therefore the mark of the "petit bourgeois" (*xiaozi*)" or "middle-class." 70s writers, with their mobility in both spaces, initially actualized and popularized this petit bourgeois imaginary. Yet eventually, due to their self-indulgence, the idea of the petit bourgeois came to be used sarcastically. Nevertheless, the role of the

Internet as the token of petit bourgeois cultural status remained an influential concept, sold in the market and the media.

As Gordon Fletcher has said, "The notion of cyberspace is an urban concept."[1] Cyberspace thrives in the social network of the urban settings and has intricate connections with real life ideologies. In this chapter, I read cyberspace as one of many urban imaginaries, a fad, and a tempting other. To do so, I explore *Xiao Yao de wang* (Xiao Yao's net) by Zhou Jieru and "Gaobie Wei'an" (Goodbye Vivian) by Anni Baobei. What emerges is a dialectic between urban and cyber spaces interlaced with themes of transgression and return.

Cyberspace and the Urban Setting

In 2000, a male publisher wanted to package some beauty writers. When he started to evaluate his candidates, his criteria was that these young writers had to have been born in the 1970s, have attended college in the 1990s, and to have come to Beijing from other provinces. They should already have published a modicum of novels and enjoyed certain fame in the media. Finally, Yan Hong, Wang Tianxiang, Luo Yijia, and Tao Sixuan were selected, and signed contracts with "Bookoo," a U.S.-based web company run by the diasporic Chinese community. Bookoo decided to publish their novels on the Internet, have them written especially for the website, and globally sell their images and writing, in both the original language and in translated versions.[2]

The episode was one of many promotional stories in the cultural marketplace exemplifying the interrelations between urban and the virtual space in that market. A beauty writer has to be young (born in the 70s). She is from a provincial area, away from her roots, her hometown and family, which means she is free from the traditional and conventional bonds.

Urban space brought young writers mobility and glamour. The virtual space expanded the reach of this mobility across the globe. It publicized their writings to a broader range of readers. The writers' market appeal implied that the public needed the cultural imagination that beauty writers represented: youth, style, mobility and glamour. Yan Hong, one of the four beauty writers, explained their cooperation with the Internet this way, "People need fast food culture... Now we cooperate with the Internet. In the future Internet fiction should be also one flower in the literary field."[3] Yan Hong regarded their Internet cooperation as a response to the public demand for popular fiction. Though the cyberspace-related fiction is "fast food" type of reading, it has the potential to break down the boundary between serious literature and pop fiction.

The "four beauty writers" episode highlighted the cultural status of the cosmopolitan city and the Internet in late 1990s in China. Both enriched the imagination of a boundary-breaking, globally related other. The city kept close contact with global opportunities through transnational companies, investment capital, and consumption. The Internet extended communication and allowed people in various urban settings to intersect. The marketability of a female writer was related to her glamour, which was enabled by her good education and physical appeal, as well as her mobility on both physical and virtual levels: her cooperation with and involvement in urban/cyber spaces. Her (acquired) urban and cyber identity and mobility embodied the fashionable imaginary of urban life: the sophisticated urban *xiaozi*. The Internet not only publicized the attractive idea of *xiaozi*, it itself was also one of many urban *xiaozi* fashions.

Cyberspace as an Urban Fashion

The major controversy concerning cyberspace focuses on the utopian and dystopian roles that the Internet plays in people's lives. The utopian view emphasizes the anywhere/anytime/anybody function of the technology-enabled cyberspace that breaks the boundaries of the social framework and enables people to realize what would be impossible in real life.[4] The dystopian view sees with dismay cyberspace's role of compartmentalizing individuals in real life. Cyberspace promotes global communication, yet when individuals make contact through the computer network rather than face-to-face, they are partially isolated and disconnected from the real world.[5] Kevin Robins and Faith Wilding demystify cyberspace and locate it in the broader social and political contexts in which cyberspace is constructed. They discover that real life issues such as racial, ethical and gender problems also exist in cyberspace.[6]

These arguments approach cyberspace from different perspectives, offering theoretical frameworks for the politics of the Internet. Nevertheless, the analysis of the "utopian, dystopian and heterotopian possibilities" of cyberspace has hitherto been made with reference to mature capitalist societies.[7] China, however, is a developing country where the market economy has only recently taken off. How should we understand the meaning of the Internet in China, where unbalanced regional growth and the wealth gap remain serious issues? What role does cyberspace play in a social context in which socialist ideology still has a powerful influence? These issues are directly related to the imaginary of cyberspace both in urban reality and in fictional narrative. To answer these questions, I would like to examine who had access to the Internet.

According to the statistics collected by China Internet Network Information Center (CNNIC) in 2000, there were 8,900,000 Internet users, 6.8% of the total population; 85.8% were young people between eighteen and thirty-five years old. Eighty-four percent had a college or higher level of education. About 66% of the Internet surfers were concentrated in the economically developed big cities in coastal areas.[8]

From the statistics, we can see that those who can regularly use the Internet constituted a small proportion of the population. The Internet was available primarily to a group of urban-based people who belonged to a culturally, financially or socially elite class. The big cities had better access to global opportunities in terms of professions, technology, and facilities. Most of the technical problems of the Internet required higher-level training, and Internet fees were relatively expensive when compared with the average income of the common people. Because of these basic requirements, it was natural that young people with higher income and college students with convenient school facilities became the major users. The majority of the former group belonged to the *xiaozi*, the latter to the potential future members of the *xiaozi*.

What exactly is the petit bourgeoisie? The definition of *xiaozi*, just as the oft-mentioned term middle class, has been quite ambiguous in China's social context. *Xiaozi* was not produced overnight. The emergence and popularity of *xiaozi* were related to three factors. The first is the de-revolutionized daily life. For the first part of the twentieth century, *xiaozi* was related to class struggle and revolutionary politics. Mao Zedong talked about "petit bourgeoisie" when he analyzed the social classes of China in 1926. The petit bourgeoisie included those "owner-peasants, the master handicraftsmen, the lower levels of the intellectuals—students, primary and secondary school teachers, lower government functionaries, office clerks, small lawyers—and small traders."[9] The petit bourgeoisie was used in opposition to peasants, the crucial class and major force of the socialist revolution, and eventually merged into the revolutionary majority. For example, after her experiences in revolutionary Yan'an, Ding Ling, who wrote such novels as "Miss Sophia's Diary," abandoned her petit bourgeois writing style and started to write proletarian novels. In the socialist classic *Qingchun zhige* (The song of youth), written by Yang Mo in 1958, the woman protagonist Lin Daojin is a petit bourgeois student. Yet she devotes herself to revolutionary work and successfully gains a new identity as a strong-willed soldier.

The concept of the petit bourgeoisie and middle class did not change until economic development and the pursuit of wealth were legitimized in the reform era. In 1982, when China was at the beginning stage of opening up and reform, Deng Xiaoping put forward a concept of the *xiaokang* society for China. *Xiaokang*, which literally means "a little affluence," refers to a well-off life. The *xiaokang* plan confirmed the pursuit of material wealth as part of the good life.

The second factor is the new urban class, such as the white-collar professionals, who emerged because of the new opportunities brought about by global capital and commercialization. The third factor is the circulation and consumption of global cultural commodities. Before it became a popular term, the media was already constructing an imaginary of alternative lifestyles and consumption. As early as the 1980s, the cultural input of Hong Kong and Taiwan songs, pulp fiction, and TV soap operas were the prelude to *xiaozi* discourse. Qiong Yao and San Mao's romantic fiction, and Teresa Teng and Luo Dayou's songs were well received in the mainland. Romantic love, exotic journeys to a foreign country, and a deliberately constructed sentiment gave evidence of a totally different imagination from the established revolutionary discourse. In the mid-1990s, "essays of little women" (*xiaonüren sanwen*) quietly began to occupy an increasingly important role in the journals and magazines. "Essay of little women" is a term mainly used with reference to a group of Guangzhou-based female writers such as Huang Aidongxi, Su Su, and Huang Yin in the early and mid-1990s. Their essays mostly focused on daily life, emotion, family, and such matters as "Paris fashion, Roman jewelry, and Chaozhou silk."[10] Meanwhile, magazines such as *Cosmopolitan*, *Rayli*, and *Elle*, with high-quality pictures, introduced detailed accounts of fashion, travel, and interior decoration.

In 1998, *Class: A Guide through the American Status System* became popular among young urbanites. In the original text, Paul Fussell critiqued social class in America and demystified the seemingly equal society. Yet in the Chinese market, the book was promoted as a "guide book for the life of white-collar people," since it contained a detailed description of the consumption-patterns and life styles of the American middle class.[11] The title of the book was translated as "*gediao*," which means taste, and the reference to social stratification was conveniently omitted. The trans-cultural (mis)reading of the text indicates a certain social demand. The original meaning of the book was appropriated or adjusted to the cultural needs of the new Chinese social group that aspired to a "better" lifestyle, characterized by "taste."

Who belonged to this new social group? Jiang Zemin, in his 2001 speech at a meeting celebrating the 80th anniversary of the founding of the CCP, mentioned the new social strata in China,

> Since China adopted the policy of reform and opening up, the composition of China's social strata has changed to some extent. There are, among others, entrepreneurs and technical personnel employed by scientific and technical enterprises of the non-public sector, managerial and technical staff employed by foreign-funded enterprises, the self-employed, private entrepreneurs, employees in intermediaries and free-

lance professionals. Moreover, many people frequently move from one ownership, sector or place to another, changing their jobs or capacity from time to time. This trend will continue.[12]

Jiang's speech formally acknowledged the emergence of the new social groups responding to the policies of reform and China's new openness, though he did not clarify the exact definition of the new class. This ambiguous political discourse, however, left room for the media to elaborate on *xiaozi* discourse.

Ge Hongbing suggests that *xiaozi* was related to desire and consumption, and it is "a life trend, a popularized life movement."[13] Bao Xiaoguang in *Xiaozi qingdiao* (Petit bourgeois taste) observes that the *xiaozi* does not have to be super rich, yet the *xiaozi's* tastes are definitely based on certain stable financial foundations. He relates *xiaozi* to the Internet, coffee, bars, the mood created by Wang Kar-wai's films, the nostalgia for the old Shanghai, Zhang Ailing, and Paris.[14] Neither Ge nor Bao give a precise definition to *xiaozi*. Most people agree that *xiaozi* share some common cultural experience and consumption styles. Generally speaking, *xiaozi* refers to a taste, a lifestyle, an imagination and a concept rather than a real class in the economic sense. Li Zhengliang summarizes *xiaozi's* cultural identifications under five categories: "urban imagination," "food," "clothes," "readings," and "visual-aural." A *xiaozi* person generally likes a big metropolis like Shanghai, Beijing, or Paris. S/he drinks coffee and likes French cuisine. His or her wardrobe is filled with brand-name clothes such as Chanel. S/he has Zhang Ailing's books on the bookshelf. S/he watches European art performances or Wang Kar-wai's films and listens to Jazz or Italian violin music.[15] Thus the cultural commodities with which *xiaozi* identify are mostly related to a cross-cultural imagination. Consuming globally-circulated commodities confirmed *xiaozi's* "taste," identity, and status, and enabled an imagined participation in global fashion.

Nevertheless, most of the Chinese population were, and still are, rural peasants and enterprise workers. *Xiaozi* occupied only a small percentage of the population. According to an academic survey, the *zhongchan jieceng* (middle-class stratum) was only 11.8% of the population.[16] Yet the term was related to such concepts of the "good, classy life" as cozy houses, cars, style, and fashion, and therefore implied a rosy ideal in the urban public imagination. The media and the commercial market sold this ideal as a tempting dream. There were many books on how to create a *xiaozi* life. Those books included *Dear Petit Bourgeoisie, Petit Bourgeois Women, Petit Bourgeois Taste: Modern Women's Life Encyclopedia* and *Petit Bourgeois Recipes*.[17]

In the urban *xiaozi* discourse, the Internet played a double role. It was a media space in which *xiaozi* fantasies were enriched and circulated. It was also one of the many *xiaozi* imaginaries. There were "*xiaozi* channels," "*xiaozi* forums" and "*xiaozi* fashions" on various websites. As I mentioned before, the

Internet was one of the facilities that the *xiaozi* possessed. The ownership of and accessibility to the cyberspace was also a token of social and cultural status. The Internet users were prosperous new urbanites who could break away from various social restraints in their cyber-communities. Being a member of the class of Internet users certified their stylish urban identity. The Internet, just like cars or houses, belonged to urban fashion (*shishang*), especially at the century's turn, when the practical functions of the Internet, such as online shopping and banking, were yet to be developed.

Writing in the Cyber/Urban Space

What did cyberspace mean for literature? Cyberspace, because of its "virtual" attributes, granted people opportunities to voice their ideas and organize communities. Everybody who had access to the Internet could post their writings on blogs, public forums and chat rooms. Such opportunities had been traditionally limited to those who could secure scarce space in newspapers or journals. This decentralized the mainstream discourse and broadened the conventional cultural and political space, hitherto largely reserved for politically approved groups. Also because of this ostensibly limit-less feature, cyberspace provided a place to create tempting fantasies of a free other.

The emergence of cyberspace as a literary medium brought new phenomena to the literary field. The Internet offered an alternative space where writers could publicize their literary identity. Seventies writers were the central constituents of the Internet surfers. Young and well educated, they were quick in responding to new technology. Some writers, such as Wei Hui, Mian Mian and Zhou Jieru, set up their own websites, and communicated with the readers through bulletin boards, chat rooms and emails.[18] Some writers, such as the four beauty writers, had their writings and pictures available on the Internet. For some *linglei* writers who could not secure a legitimate space in the conventional literary journals and publishing houses, virtual space became the only way for them to make their novels and writings available to readers. After *Shanghai Baby* and *Candy* were banned, millions of curious readers clicked on various links of the web pages to have a peek at these controversial novels. Some writers were directly engaged in writing and publishing novels on the Internet. A large group of "Internet writing fellows" (*xieshou*), such as Anni Baobei, Li Xunhuan, Nin Caishen, and Xing Yusen, to name a few, surfaced. They enjoyed certain popularity among regular web surfers, and their writings were widely read across the Internet.

Cyberspace also offered an alternative way, a shortcut to some extent, for people to approach the mainstream literary space and acquire a literary identity. A website, www.rongshu.com, created by an American Chinese named

Xiangzi, is a space for people to post their creative original writings. The creator and editors of "rongshu.com" proudly announce the "rongshu" website as a repository of "global Chinese original works."[19] Literary success in cyberspace had a real-world impact on writers' lives and literary careers. For example, Anni Baobei started her writing career on the Internet. Without the support of any commercial promotion, her writings became popular among Internet surfers, and won her attention from publishers and the opportunity to publish her writings in print media. As cyber writing became more and more popular, publishers collected writings from the Internet and compiled them into books. Zhishi chubanshe (Knowledge publishing house) brought forth the "E-age" series. Chunfeng wenyi chubanshe (Spring breeze publishing house) tried to discover new novelists through the Internet and compiled the "Youth, Love" series. Zhongguo wenlian chubanshe (Chinese Literature Association) also had published selected works of the new age cyber-fiction.[20]

As more and more writing emerged over the Internet, the term "Internet literature" (*wangluo wenxue*), or cyber-writing, came into view. It is very vague what kind of writings can be labeled Internet fiction. According to *Zhongguo dangdai wenxueshi* (History of contemporary Chinese literature), "Internet fiction" includes three categories: conventional literary works that are scanned and placed on the Internet, writings that are enabled by the technologies and Internet (such as hyperlink-packed articles), and writings that are directly written for and publicized on the Internet.[21]

Literary critics responded to the new form of writing differently. Ge Hongbing gave high marks to cyber-writing and its social role of giving more people the chance to express themselves and have fun.[22] As a literary historian, Chen Pingyuan was more reserved and expressed his suspicions. He preferred to use the term "literature of the Internet age." According to him, the Internet provides a new medium for the publication and dissemination of writings. The technology-enabled free expression is fast, convenient, and accessible, but does not necessarily have "the aesthetic of writings" (*wenzhang de meigan*), which takes people years to achieve in the conventional development of print writers. Chen was obviously concerned with the classic meaning of literature. For him, the Internet enables a fantasy of writing, but not the real, classic literature.[23]

Both Chen and Ge recognized the free expression enabled by cyber space. Indeed, the Internet has, to some extent, revolutionized conventional literature, as more people can publicize their writings. Nevertheless, as I have argued, the Internet was related to petit bourgeois practice. Only certain social groups, such as white-collar professionals or college students, had regular access. The expansion of literary spaces, revolutionary as it is, had its limitations as well.

Because cyberspace offered the rosy illusion of a seemingly free community, it became an escapist fantasy. Cyberspace fantasy provided an imagined mobility and communication, yet unintentionally kept urbanites away from the reality around them. The ambiguous balance between the cyber illusion and urban reality became an intriguing topic for writers. To explore the fictional narrative of the Internet as an easy escape, I will examine closely *Xiao Yao's Net* written by Zhou Jieru, and "Goodbye, Vivian" by Anni Baobei. Both novels were written in 2000.

Regarded as the first Internet novel written by a professional writer, *Xiao Yao's Net* is a story of a young woman's journey in cyber/urban space.[24] The protagonist's cyber/urban space flight embodies the urbanites' balance between escape (an inspiration to the intangible cyber other) and return (an awareness of self as a member of a larger community). "Goodbye Vivian" is about a man's displaced, and therefore tragic, fantasy in the dual reality of the urban and the cyber worlds. It is typical cyber-writing, since it was originally written and publicized on the Internet. It is also a typical *xiaozi* text as it is filled with a detailed description of the urban lifestyle. Nevertheless, Anni Baobei demystified a common *xiaozi* fantasy by bringing to light the ugly truth behind the rosy veneer of the cyber/urban illusion.

Xiao Yao's Net: The Inescapable Real/Virtual Nets

Born in 1976, Zhou Jieru was one of the seventies writers who made their collective debut in *Writer* in 1998. She quit her job in a local government institute and became a professional writer. *Xiao Yao's Net* centers on I-narrator Ruru's double life in urban space and cyberspace. "Xiao Yao," which literally means "little demon," is one of many cyber names that the twenty-four-year-old woman Ruru uses to frequent the Internet chat rooms. There are two "nets" in Xiao Yao's life, literally and figuratively: one is the real life net that involves her office job in a local government department, her loving parents who expect her to have a stable and normal life, and her unsuccessful love affairs with men. The other is the Internet, cyberspace, where Ruru, using various names, surfs the web and meets people online. Xiao Yao connects the two nets together by befriending and dating Internet pals she meets in the online chat rooms. Straddling the two spaces, Ruru is looking for a carefree lifestyle and devoted love relationship in urban/cyber reality.

Ruru is bothered by her self-created problems in daily life, and she tries to break away from the complicated nets of reality. She regards her government job, which many people envy, as a restriction on her individual freedom. Her parents are old-fashioned in her eyes, and she constantly has conflicts with them. Meanwhile, cyberspace seemingly grants her unlimited freedom to explore various alternative lifestyles. Free from any social roles in cyberspace, she does not need to be a well-behaved civil servant or a good daughter who follows the rules all the time. She is her own person on the Internet. She can play whatever roles she wants, take whatever persona she wishes, and freely develop friendships with people she likes. For her, the Internet is a boundary-breaking interconnected new world at her fingertips. She says, "The net is a small society. What I face is not a group of people, a city, a country, but the whole world."[25] In the cyberspace community, she drifts from one chat room to another and meets numerous people from different places and countries. Like her, they are hidden in various identities and looking for freedom and excitement. She innocently believes that she can get away from the troubles and problems of the human network so long as she plugs in a telephone line and surfs the Internet. She says,

> I wish I had been born in 2000. When I open my eyes, I will see a world made up of computers and the Internet. All the evil concepts will be deleted, and all the good ideas will be upgraded. All the relations, such as that of parents and children, men and women, people and people, will become simple.[26]

After Ruru's relation with her supervisors and her parents sour, she chooses to escape from her real-life problems. She quits the job that her father has arranged for her, leaves her home, rents her own apartment, and organizes her life in the way she likes. Instead of looking for solutions in reality, she spends her days taking trips and surfing the Internet. Air travel brings her to cities in faraway places. Cyberspace community enables more opportunities. Both provide the imaginary of easy escape in the air, thereby attracting Ruru's attention. She travels from city to city, meeting her cyber friends and lovers. Her floating identity, embodied through her mobility in both space (the urban and the Internet), implies that she is not tied down. For her, going to distant spaces is an easy solution to her problems.

Zhou Jieru is not the only writer who centers on the theme of escape on the road. Other writers of her generation are fascinated by the mobility of urban spaces. Novels such as "Go to Shanghai" (Zhu Wenying), "Start out from Nanjing" (Wei Wei) and "Live in Ailin" (Ma Li) highlight writers/protagonists' desire to escape from immediate reality. In "Go to Shanghai," the protagonist Yiwei has a romantic image of Shanghai, and this poetic feeling drives her to the city. To feed that feeling, she often goes to Shanghai to shop for clothes. She feels her rendezvous in Shanghai shorten her distance from the city. "Starting out from Nanjing" deals with a couple's journey to different cities. Starting out from Nanjing, the protagonists go to Shijiazhuang, Beijing, and Tianjin. Yet they are constantly disappointed by the cities, and eventually return to Nanjing, the place where they start, the downtrodden city from which they try to escape. To them, life is like a circle from which they cannot escape. "Live in Ailin" is about an illusionary city Ailin, a city that people cannot locate on the map. Yet it is a city to which an exhausted traveler goes, a city that people can see at night when all the lights are on, a city that the I-narrator reads about in a book. In a word, it is a metaphorical city, an alternative city space that derives from the writer's pure imagination.

For Ruru, one attractive opportunity that faraway cyberspace provides is romance, or the imagination of romance. She encounters new friends in cyberspace, and locates romance in a distant reality. She claims,

> I don't talk about deep questions. I won't participate in the seventy-two-hour cyberspace survival experiment. I won't attend the Miss Internet Pageant. I don't understand e-business. Nor do I manage an online bookstore. What I do is to date online.[27]

To actualize her cyber-love, Ruru flies to various cities to date her lovers. The men involved in her life are nicknamed "Peace," "Health" and "Happiness," embodying Ruru's good wishes. On the road, she finds out she is not alone in commuting to bring an invisible romance into reality. She observes "(m)ore and more beautiful girls will go to cyberspace. More and more beautiful girls will get tired of reality. In the end, the Internet becomes the only life, the trend of the future."[28]

Does cyberspace really become more real than the real life? By analyzing the "cyberpunk texts," Marjorie Worthington argues that although cyberspace offers people freedom to escape the physical, it is the physical body that is translated into cyberspace. Therefore, the physical body has the power to influence the cyber body.[29] Though cyberspace provides Ruru with the power to inhabit a self of her own creation in a boundary-free community, her real-life self constantly intervenes into her cyber freedom. Cyberspace does not liberate her from the reality after all. Those with whom she interacts, either in real space and cyberspace, are still real people.

The real and the virtual affect each other. Ruru cannot tell what is real and what is not. To highlight the blurred boundary, the writer uses both cyberlanguage and traditional language in the novels.[30] Some Internet signs, such as "^_*", are used in the text. Real-life crises are shifted into cyberspace. She fights with people in the chat room, just as in real life. Meanwhile, cyberspace illusions are also brought into reality. Her cyberspace personalities influence her real-life behavior. The love affairs she carries out online eventually end up in real life. Her self-centered pursuit of freedom hurts the feelings of her parents. Ruru realizes that the Internet is a *fin de siècle* "spiritual opium." As her friend tells her,

> I said I like the Internet. But we are in reality, not the Internet. Even though we see a

lot of short-lived love on the Internet and the cyber love is right beside us, it has nothing to do with us.[31]

Ruru is caught in both "nets" when she tries to break free from all restrictions. Her independence proves vulnerable. She cannot deal with even her poorly equipped apartment. At the end of the story, Ruru's parents are involved in a crime attempt and badly injured, and Ruru realizes she cannot leave her family. She decides to return home, live with her parents, and start a new life again in reality.

Xiao Yao's Net was based on Zhou Jieru's own experiences with the Internet. Zhou even used her own cyber-name "Ruru" as the name of the I-narrator. Ruru's cyber/urban escape flows from her aspiration to free life and true love, which turns out to be an illusion in cyberspace. The Internet is associated with reality. Since the escape is groundless, it is doomed to fail. Ruru eventually returns to her home, fulfilling a cultural relocation to the initial space. Zhou Jieru also decided to quit the Internet. What she loves, Zhou said, is reality.[32]

Anni Baobei: *Xiaozi* in Cyber/urban Space

Zhou Jieru's cyberspace escape and urban return is expressed through a fictional narrative. The fantasy created by Anni Baobei herself and her texts, however, was disseminated as *xiaozi* imagination in real life. Since both the Internet writers and readers were related more or less to *xiaozi*, cyberspace writings were developed to meet the cultural and emotional needs of this group of people, which explains the great popularity of Anni Baobei's online novels among Internet users, for nothing better embodied the relation between the Internet and *xiaozi* imagery than her initial online writings.   Not only are the protagonists in Anni Baobei's writings the well-mannered city-dwellers who frequent shopping malls and office buildings, or other modern urban spaces, but the writer herself displays "good taste" in her choice of music, ice cream and casual dress.

Anni Baobei, the cyber/pen name of Li Jie, is always related to cyber writing. She started her writing career online. Her novels, such as "Goodbye Vivian" and *Flowers at the Distant Shore* (Bi'an hua), are full of typical *xiaozi* images and themes. A girl always wears a white cotton dress, with her bare feet in sneakers and silver bracelets on her wrist. A woman is seen in a short-sleeved, embroidered silk *qipao* and her shoulders are wrapped in a pure wool scarf with tassels. The coffee is not ordinary coffee; it is either cappuccino with cinnamon or Italian double espresso. The residence is not an ordinary house; its architecture is European and it is landscaped with parasol trees. The car is not merely a vehicle for transportation; it is a black BMW with a special plate designating its owner as foreign.

Anni Baobei admitted that she had more passion for materials than people.[33] Her novels can be read as handbooks for *xiaozi*, teaching people what is really "classy" and how to have "taste." The online discussion on Anni Baobei goes, "Wanna be a *xiaozi*? Read Anni Baobei's writings."[34] The *xiaozi* materials, mood, and sentiment, constructed in the fictional narrative, were popularized through cyberspace and attracted many readers online. When *Goodbye Vivian* was published as a book, it was well received in the market. Within two years, the book had been printed twice.[35] Anni Baobei herself also became a cultural icon, a young (post)modern urban woman whose identity involved many qualities that urbanites admired: a free-lance writer (which hints at freedom and a good income) and elegant connoisseur (which suggests good taste).

"Goodbye Vivian" is a cyber romance.[36] White-collar professional Lin is attracted by a somewhat mysterious girl named Vivian in an online chat room. In the subway station of the city where he lives, he meets a girl in a black T-shirt whom he believes is Vivian. Meanwhile, out of loneliness he and his colleague Qiao have an affair. For a while, his cyber/urban, virtual/real, romances are balanced. He keeps a vague good feeling towards both cyber Vivian and urban Vivian, and detaches himself from his real affair with Qiao. The balance is destroyed when Qiao becomes pregnant and Lin refuses to make any commitment. Qiao commits suicide out of desperation. Her death drives Lin to question himself and seek out the true identities of both cyber/urban Vivian. The elegant subway girl, the urban Vivian, turns out to be a drug-addict and the mistress of a married rich man. The online Vivian reveals the truth that she lives in a faraway city and she does not want to meet Lin in person because she wants to keep the beautiful feeling of their cyber relationship forever. Lin's cyber/urban fantasy collapses. He has to leave both Vivians as well as the city where he lives.

The two "Vivians" embody the dialectical relation between the real and the unreal, the near and the distant, symbolizing a cyber/urban fantasy as well as objects of male desire. The cyber Vivian provides a virtual connection to distant places, the possibility of mobility, and a potential virtual adventure. The male protagonist's Internet romance moves him away from his immediate reality. The urban Vivian, a girl often seen in the subway, entices the male character to explore the metropolis. The urban scenes, such as the subway, office building, coffee house, and apartment, constitute each individual scene in the narrative, highlighting the melancholy urbanites and their ambiguous desires. In Lin's life, the two Vivians are more real in his self-absorbed reality. He is obsessed with his daily online chat with one Vivian and his urban en-counters with the other. The loneliness, melancholy and sentiment as well as various modern urban images are the trademarks of Anni Baobei's writings. They are the symbols with which the urban petit bourgeoisie people identify with both culturally and emotionally.

Since neither Vivians is real, the male fantasy of a cyber/urban Vivian cannot be fulfilled. The pessimistic ending demystifies a cyber/urban fantasy: as the protagonist pursues the intangible, he loses what is at hand, and eventually, his whole city reality. The mental attachment to the distant "other" enabled by cyberspace and detachment from the reality were the common attributes of urban *xiaozi*. As one critic commented, what *xiaozi* liked were the "past tense" and the "future tense."[37] The former includes some deliberately created nostalgia, such as Shanghai of the 1930s, when Shanghai then was Westernized; and the latter refers to the aspiration to share in the grandeur of economically advanced foreign countries, embodied by foreign-brand commodities. It is the future tense because luxury consumption was not common at a time when the majority of the Chinese population was still concerned with the basic problems of living. The *xiaozi*'s taste was built on the imagination of the "other" and the obsession of self in an imagined community. Since they ignored the "here" and "now" reality, the *xiaozi* was criticized as narcissistic, self-centered, pretentious, and vain.

Nevertheless, the *xiaozi* still remains an attractive image in the media and the commercial market. Starbuck's Coffee is seen on the corners of major Chinese cities. Foreign-branded commodities sell well. Online romance still goes on, and becomes more and more possible. Anni Baobei let her protagonist Lin fail as an urban *xiaozi*, since he is too obsessed with the unreal. Yet Anni herself is very successful as a token of *xiaozi*. At least, that is how she and her cyber writings are packaged in the urban market. Anni Baobei's success proves that the virtual is not only closely related to reality, but that it changes reality.

Though the protagonists in Zhou Jieru and Anni Baobei's stories fail in their cyber/urban adventures, the meaning of the Internet as an alternative literary space is far-reaching. Karen Cadora argues that cyberpunk literature is an important tool for the empowerment of the individual (especially the feminist) because it has the potential to envision "fragmented subjects who can, despite their multiple positioning, negotiate and succeed in a high-tech world."[38] In terms of high-tech space success, female writers expanded their literary space from the real to the virtual, from urban to cyber. It should come as no surprise that their writings succeeded as both urban fashion and alternative literature, which posed a serious challenge to the conventional, elitist concept of "literature." This tension is my focal point in the next chapter.

CHAPTER FOUR

Glamorously Intellectual: An Intertextual Reading of Wei Hui

Wei Hui was arguably the most controversial literary figure at the end of 1999. By her explicit treatment of female sexuality, she dissolved the boundaries of the elite and the popular, the moral and the decadent. This transgressiveness in writing, morality, and convention, in both her fiction and her life, caused wide-scale anxiety over the corruption of the literary and moral establishment, and made her one of the most controversial female writers of her generation. According to Wei Hui, the media has turned "Wei Hui" into a cultural code and a demonized image, which is not the real her.[1] The name "Wei Hui" itself is also related to erotica and decadence. If so, what kind of social and cultural psychology does "Wei Hui" reflect in literature and the media? If the *real* Wei Hui is not the media representation of Wei Hui, as she herself claims, how can we understand the discrepancy?[2]

In this chapter, I will examine the inter-textuality of the female writer and her texts by reading Wei Hui and her novels, and evaluate Wei Hui's status as a "writer-cum-star," and her positioning of herself as the glamorous intellectual. For though the media has played an important role in the construction of her scandalous identity, she was by no means a passive object, actively participating, as she did, in the making of herself as a cultural symbol.

A "spokesperson" of the Newly-new generation, Wei Hui identified with city spectacles, the market, and material pleasure. Yet she also consciously differentiated herself from other beauties by stressing her academic background. Her literary identity in popular veneer made her a morally and culturally ambiguous figure. Her performance as a star in the cultural market brought her fame, glamour, profit and transnational mobility. It is also her high-profile image in the market and her openness towards desire and sexuality that upset the public and eventually turned a commercial showcase into a political sensation when her book was banned in mainland markets. Though certainly not the first female writer to articulate female sexuality, Wei Hui has become particularly controversial because of her self-promotion and her "writing of desire" (*yuwang hua xiezuo*).[3]

Most of Wei Hui's stories written in the late 1990s have a woman writer as the central character and writing as the central theme. "Becoming a writer" is a common motif. The basic storylines are similar: a young, literarily talented Fudan University graduate lives in Shanghai, works on a writing project, and eventually realizes her dream at certain emotional cost. Between the gray zone of the fiction and the autobiography, the imaginary of female spiritual/physical desire is articulated in the global/local context. Nevertheless, what Wei Hui constructed textually is a female fantasy of a new cosmopolitan life not yet hers. Once the imagined global mobility had been realized through her writing, Wei Hui started her cultural journey back home.

Wei Hui, the penname of Zhou Weihui, graduated from Fudan University. She has been often labeled a *linglei* writer. What exactly was the *linglei*? Wei Hui's words might have something to say on the conception of a Newlynew generation female writer:

> It is very lucky to be a woman writer in *fin de siècle* China. Those models, singers, hair stylist, painters, agents, idle punk, bald financial analyst, and I are the most material and the most progressive insects who secretly exist by eating the city.[4]

Taking the city as an object of consumption, Wei demystified writing as one of many urban professions, materially based and desire charged, rather than as a serious literary engagement. A female writer is a progressive urbanite, actualizing her desire through writing and consuming the city.

As Wei Hui presented herself, in both real life and in her texts, as a glamorous writer-cum-star, she was inevitably consumed by the mass media, the commercial market, and the global public. She was gazed upon, judged and marketed in the global market. Ironically, the mass consumption of beauty (female writers) and writing (texts) was also what Wei Hui expected and anticipated in her fictional narrative.

The Negotiation of the Elite and the Popular

It is important to situate Wei Hui in the cultural background against which the status of the elite, the high-brow (*ya*) culture, and the popular, the low-brow (*su*) was changing. The change was partially due to the (postmodern) attempt to re-evaluate the institutionalized grand narrative of literary history in academia, and partially because of the global consumer culture and its presence in the local cultural market.

The *ya/su* negotiation, according to Chen Pingyuan, was an important perspective in cultural development throughout 20th century China.[5] For political reasons, it was always the elite literature that dominated the writing of mainstream literary history. At the beginning of the twentieth century, prose fiction was assigned the grand mission of saving the nation. In the 1980s, literature epitomized knowledge and hence power in the post-Cultural Revolution "high culture fever."[6] Popular fiction had been dismissed as reflecting low-grade taste and triviality, and therefore remained invisible within the mainstream literary narrative.

Chen was not alone in promoting the legitimate status of popular texts. In 1995, Yan Jiayan, a Beijing University professor, included Jin Yong's martial arts novels in the college curriculum.[7] In 1996, Xie Mian termed Cui Jian's rock'n'roll song lyric as "cultural classics" along with the works of big names such as Shu Ting, Bei Dao, and many other novelists.[8] In 1998, Qian Liqun, Wen Rumin and Wu Fuhui incorporated pop fiction, which includes "mandarin duck and butterfly" novels and martial arts fiction, into the literary history of modern Chinese literature in *Zhongguo xiandai wenxue sanshi nian* (Thirty years of modern Chinese literature).[9]

In the commercial market and public media, the popular text was an efficient way to attract profits, as most of the cultural and media institutes were made responsible for their own profit and loss, and their cultural products were delivered over to the "invisible hand" of the market. Pure literature journals faced the problems of losing readership in the 1990s. Pressured by their immediate survival crisis, many pure literature journals started to adjust themselves to popular taste and change their strategies to appeal to readers and consumers. Journals such as *Hunan wenxue* (Hunan literature), *Huanghe* (Yellow river), *Xiaoshuo jia* (Novelist), and *Qingnian wenxue* (Youth literature) changed their original elite style and included popular content. In 1998, the editors of *Beijing wenxue* (Beijing literature) announced that novels should be "pleasant to read" (*haokan*), clarifying its attempt to attract readers. To make the journal pleasant to read, editors added new columns such as its "popular forum" (*baijia zhengyan*). Scholars and experts were invited to argue on cultural topics such as TV soap operas, and high school language and literature education. *Writer* transformed itself from a journal to a more popular magazine. Changing the journal's name to *Writer's Magazine* (Zuojia zazhi), the editors made an ambitious plan to make the magazine the "Chinese version of the *New Yorker*." Editor-in-chief Zong Renfa claimed that what the editors did was to "try to pull the journal out of the 'narrow road' of pure literature, and move literature away from its narcissistic indulgence."[10]

The practice of these literary journals caused much controversy. Taiwan writer Zhang Dachun, for example, expressed his concern over vulgarized literature. According to Zhang, pure literature journals aim to challenge readers aesthetically and prepare them for new literary experiences. Yet if "pleasant to read" becomes the standard by which editors evaluate novels and promote journals to readers, it would discourage experimentation in more progressive literary styles.[11]

Nevertheless, both the elite and the popular continued to play against each other. Pop songs, TV soap operas, and pulp fiction were put into new perspective both commercially and academically. Also, serious literature and popular fiction writers were learning to keep a close relation to the market. The emergence of "beauty writers" highlighted the contestation of the elite and the popular. On the one hand, female writers restored and also revised the sensational effect of literature. In the 1980s, various literary trends, such as scar literature, root-searching literature or avant-guard literature initiated new rounds of cultural exploration. However, literature lost its sensational appeal during the 1990s, as the cultural market was geared towards more entertaining genres such as TV soap operas, films and games. Novels were no longer the only texts available for people to consume. Just as the literary journals suffered the loss of readers and profits, young women writers bought in a new style. The urban life they constructed in the fiction presented a different literary imaginary. An editor of a literary journal revealed that the journal received more and more readers' letters that were addressed to Wei Hui and others, though the overall number of readers' letters had decreased dramatically.[12]

Against the backdrop of a "vulgarized" high culture or the elevated status of popular culture, Wei Hui chose to present herself as a figure of glamorous intelligence or intellectual glamour, a member and exemplar of the Newly-newmetropolitan humanity. Her strategy of being cool and literarily talented appealed both to the market and the literary world. Her playing with high and low culture and her zeal for both material and spiritual gains are embodied in the image of a writer that she presented in the market and the persona of the writer that she projected in the texts.

Elite Identity in Popular Text: Intertextual Readings of Wei Hui and Her Novels

Wei Hui's three novels, "Crazy Like Wei Hui," *Shanghai Baby* and "Pistol of Desire," all involve a girl who writes novels and becomes a stylishly success-ful writer in the city. In these texts on "becoming a writer," Wei designed her film star-like literary career. Ironically, the texts were like a prophecy: they foretold what happened later to Wei Hui in real life. By being actively in-volved in a story-line that derives from both the real and the fabricated, Wei Hui announced and realized her ideal of being a beautiful writer-cum-star.

The storylines of the aforementioned novels are similar: an ambitious young female protagonist tries to become famous through writing, and meanwhile is emotionally involved with men. "Crazy Like Wei Hui" has "Wei Hui" as the main character. Wei Hui is writing a novel and looking for publishers. Meanwhile, she and her girlfriend explore the metropolis and meet various people. *Pistol of Desire* recounts the growing-up of a girl named Mini. Mini breaks away from her dysfunctional family and alcoholic father, advances to Fudan University, and starts her journey of writing and dating. *Shanghai Baby* centers on the triangular relation between Coco, the main character, and her effeminate Chinese boyfriend and hyper-masculine German lover, while she is writing a "masterpiece" that can make her famous.

In *Shanghai Baby*, I-narrator Coco declares her ambition: "I am twenty-five, and I want to be a writer. Even though the profession's totally passé, I am going to make writing up-to-date again." [13] Coco's words highlight the changing meaning of writing. Though writing as an intellectual activity is falling out of favor, it could acquire a new glamorous appeal, when undertaken by a young, smart urban woman who is good at playing with both words and reality. Coco frankly reveals her pursuit of fame: "Every morning when I open my eyes I wonder what I can do to make myself famous. It's become my ambition, almost my rasion d'être, to burst upon the city like fireworks."[14]

In *Crazy Like Wei Hui*, a male publisher tells the I-narrator Wei Hui how to design her literary reputation:

> How is that, Miss Wei? Your first book will be a hot best-seller. Your readers will be those who are between fourteen and forty years old. You can hold some book-signing events in major cities, with a charming smile on your face. Your huge picture will be hung at the most showy spot in the book market. You will be like a real beauty writer, a genius writer.[15]

In fact, Wei Hui did use various ways to promote herself as a high-profile attractive star, as she planned in her novels. For example, she printed her portrait and passages from "Crazy Like Wei Hui" on men's underwear and put it on display in an art exhibition.[16] Her books did sell well. *Shanghai Baby* was first printed in September 1999. By the following March, it had been reprinted seven times.[17] Wei's pictures were sold along with these books. In the pictures, Wei, in different clothes and hair styles, poses like a movie star. She did make writers and writings "popular again" by adopting such concepts as beauty writer and body writing. These new and sensational terms injected into writing the sense of fashion and eroticism, and therefore became saturated with market appeal and moral controvesy.

For Coco in *Shanghai Baby*, the promotion of writing is like a masquerade:

> My dream is one that any smart young woman would have, and that's the kind of person I am writing for. There should be a road show with parties throughout China to promote the book. I'd wear a backless black dress and a grotesque mask. The floor would be littered with confetti made from my book, and everyone would be dancing madly on it.[18]

Among many possible interpretations, I read the confetti of the book as the symbol of the falling of writing. Writing becomes a visual spectacle, an opportunity for the protagonist to fulfill her longings for fun, fame and material wealth, and a culturally narcissistic gesture. When Wei Hui turns writing-related activity into a masquerade, writing becomes the consumption of style and pleasure. A once-intellectual activity becomes a carnival, in which the writer gains a chance to show herself off like a stylishly clad star.

Though Wei Hui identified with the pop star and mass consumption of the material, pleasure, and desire, she also constantly referred to the fact that she was a graduate of Fudan University, a prestigious academic institute. Because of her educational background, she consciously differentiated herself from other writers, such as Mian Mian, who did not make it through high school. Wei said, "I think the new woman should have a high level of education and also be interesting. Plus, I have serious prejudice about higher education. I only make friends with those who have it."[19] "Fudan University" is always mentioned in various introductions in the media and the market. In the English version of *Shanghai Baby*, Wei Hui dedicates the book to her "parents," "love" and "Fudan University."[20] Her academic background added intellectual glamour to her image in the popular market.

Wei Hui was proud of the fact that she embraces different cultures. She claimed, "My lifestyle is very Westernized. I worked as a coffee house waitress. I chat with customers in fluent English. I watch foreign films, read foreign books in the original. I can speak some German, and want to study French. I hope I can write in foreign languages one day." [21] Her pride in her knowledge of foreign cultures can be seen in Wei's treatment of her text. In *Shanghai Baby*, for each chapter, she quotes western philosophers or intellectuals such Sigmund Freud, Henry Miller, Milan Kundera, Nietzsche and others. Meanwhile, she also draws lines from Elizabeth Taylor, Marilyn Monroe, Paul Simon, Madonna and other pop stars. The quoted lines of feminism, post-colonialism, and psychoanalysis give the popular text a seeming touch of high culture. The play of the foreign high and popular culture supplies a sense of the other, as well as a touch of stylishness.

As Wei Hui said, "My ideal literary work should have profound intellectual content and a best-selling, sexy cover,"[22] and she designed her literary position accordingly. Her academic, cultured identity and her market-oriented attitude attested to the blurry boundary between high and low cultures. Her self-positioning as a "serious" writer in popular form challenged the conventional identity of a demure, intellectual writer, and made her flexible in adjusting to both the elite and the popular.

The Dual Role of Subject/Object

In *Shanghai Baby*, Coco's zeal for fame and attention is reminiscent of Zhang Ailing in the 1930s. For Zhang, fame "should come as soon as possible," because "if fame arrives late, my pleasure will not be as great."[23] In her study of Zhang Ailing's self-commoditization in the 1930s, Janet Ng argues that self-commodification enables a woman to be a subject and an object at the same time, as she is the very person who markets herself. This defies the usual gender line, with men being the active subjects and women the objects.[24]

The dual role of subject/object also fits Wei Hui. Wei actively participated in the making of herself and bringing her book into the spotlight. She is created and also creating herself as a stylish writer. Take *Shanghai Baby* as an example. Wei had photos taken of the characters people had inscribed on her naked skin. After the book was published, she went to major cities, attended book-signing events and promoted her book. She had her book translated and sold in transnational markets. She traveled to America and Europe, doing TV interviews and lectures. She fulfilled her ambitious plan of becoming a glamorous writer who enjoyed mobility and public attention.

Wei Hui's self-promotion made her one of the hottest stars. It was also her excessive self-promotion that led to the ban of *Shanghai Baby* and her more or less self-exile. When she promoted *Shanghai Baby* in Chengdu, the local tabloid published a picture of her wearing a revealing dress and claimed that Wei wanted people to "see the breasts of the Shanghai baby."[25] This annoyed government officials. *Shanghai Baby* was banned on the grounds that it was of "low-grade content and taste."[26] The publishing house, Chunfeng wenyi chubanshe, made a public announcement and burned all the copies, and in Beijing, Shanghai, Huzhou, and Chengdu, *Shanghai Baby* was confiscated as an illegal book.

Nevertheless, the ban only enhanced Wei's popularity, invited more curious readers to click on the Internet links, and multiplied pirated versions of the book. The official taboo was secretly appropriated for business promotion. Other than the pirated version of *Shanghai Baby*, books with titles such as "Beijing baby," "Guangzhou baby," and "super baby" were seen in the hands of private book sellers, turning the ban itself into a show.

Ironically, the response from the market was also what Wei Hui expected. She even anticipated readers' voyeuristic gaze and critical attitudes. In *Crazy Like Wei Hui*, she predicted her readership this way:

I noticed three men of different ages. The old guy, with his serious expression, bought the book to seek a target for his attack. The half-bald middle aged man, eyes behind glasses, bought this book to satisfy his voyeuristic thirst. The young man's expression was exuberant. He moved his neck like a male horse and showered me with flattering words. For him, this book was like a boxing game, a strong spirit, and a girl.[27]

Wei created herself and her readers. Actively expecting and confronting their gaze, Wei Hui established, in the texts and in the market, an energetic female subjectivity, which speaks of female desire: a longing to be a physically and spiritually fulfilled cosmopolitan citizen moving freely in the global/local context.

Shanghai Baby: Female City and Female Desire

A woman's personal fantasy of an ideal life and social position in the dazzling metropolis is best embodied in *Shanghai Baby*. The title *Shanghai Baby* implies the relation between the city and the woman. Wei Hui said, "No other city can be related to a baby. Being a baby means being pretty, spoiled, and admired, very feminine. Only Shanghai can be called a baby. "[28]

Wei Hui was among many female writers who were infatuated with the cultural reconstruction of Shanghai in the late 1990s. Chen Danyan wrote a series of "Shanghai books:" *Shanghai de feng hua xue yue* (Shanghai's breeze, flower, snow and moon), *Shanghai de jingzhi yuye* (Shanghai princess) and *Shanghai de hongyan yishi* (Shanghai beauty). These popular, photo-laden books recalled the cosmopolitan Shanghai of the first half of the twentieth century, and culturally constructed Shanghai as a feminine figure. Wang Anyi also recounted the life of Wang Qiyao, a former Miss Shanghai, in her novel *Chang hen ge* (The song of everlasting sorrow) and narrated Shanghai history between the 1940s and the 1980s in detailed daily accounts. In women's writings, Shanghai became a female figure, attentively engaging ordinary, daily rhythms interspersed with momentary shining moments of being young and vibrant.[29] Women became the center of the writing and unfolded another perspective of the city's history.

Wei Hui also detached herself from the grand narrative of the city and rewrote the story of the city with women as the focus. She constructed a female space to articulate female anxiety, desire and ideals as well as female subjectivity. The female-dominated narrative is evident in Wei Hui's stories. It is the male characters who eventually disappear. In *Crazy Like Wei Hui*, protagonist Wei Hui maintains an on-and-off relationship with her lover. Towards the end, her lover vanishes from her life. *Pistol of Desire* ends as Mini's father dies and her lovers leave her. In all of these stories, the young, beautiful, and agitated female protagonist explores her identity and sexuality through men. She enjoys the spiritual and physical pleasure but meanwhile maintains her independence. Nevertheless, though the male's disappearance always leaves her bewildered and disoriented, his absence leaves Shanghai a feminine space in the female narrative.

The feminine Shanghai in the *fin de siècle* becomes a seductive and erotic "baby" in *Shanghai Baby*. Wei Hui's feminine Shanghai is invested with the pleasure of consumption and eroticism. Both the city and city dwellers favor a hedonistic lifestyle. The female protagonist Coco, a semi-self of Wei Hui, is a "Shanghai baby," being young, sexy, and attractive. As a writer, Coco is highly aware of the opportunity that *fin de siècle* Shanghai provides if she wants to let herself and her writings become glamorous:

> My instinct told me that I should write about turn-of-the-century Shanghai. This fun-loving city: the bubbles of happiness that rise from it, the new generation it has nurtured, and the vulgar, sentimental, and mysterious atmosphere to be found in its back streets and alleys. This is a unique Asian city. Since the 1930s it has preserved a culture where China and the West met intimately and evolved together, and now it has entered its second wave of westernization.[30]

The nostalgic colonial memory and euphoric embrace of Westernization confirm Coco's infatuation with Shanghai's West-related cosmopolitan past and the current resuscitation of the exotic other. The liaison with the west, "the second wave of Westernization," brings in new fun, materials, and opportunities to the city as well as the ambitious "babies," to the city.

Though the city is presented as a feminine baby, it has no lack of phallic symbols. When Coco observes the city at night, she reflects on the city this way,

> Standing on the roof, we looked at the silhouettes of the buildings lit up by the streetlights on both sides of the Huangpu River, especially the Oriental Pearl TV Tower, Asia's tallest. Its long, long steel column pierces the sky, proof of the city's phallic worship.[31]

Yet, the phallic/masculine part of the city is less a patriarchal threat than a consumable pleasure. In the libidinal consumption of the city, Coco is involved in triangular affairs with two men: her impotent Chinese boyfriend Tian Tian and hyper-masculine German lover Mark. The flesh versus soul game is intertwined with Coco's ambitious project of writing an extraordinary novel so that she can "burst upon the city like fireworks."[32] Meanwhile, Coco also experiences various aspects of Shanghai's (post)modern life. Her "firework" dream betrays her ambition to enjoy the city, go beyond the city, and glamorize the city and herself. She takes full advantage of the culture "where China and the West met intimately." She frequents new urban spaces such as bars, shopping centers, night clubs and art galleries. She hangs around with cool urbanites such as the white-collar professionals, hair designers, editors, filmmakers, artists and a mysterious rich widow.

Coco's love affair is often read as a "weak-China" (emasculated Tian Tian) vs. "strong-West" (hyper-masculine Mark), a national allegory often seen in literary writing ever since the May Fourth era. Coco surrenders herself to Western power, as exemplified by Mark. Because of this, Wei Hui was criticized as embracing the decadent mentality of servility. Responding to this type of criticism, Wei said, "I am shocked and scared that my book could be related to such grand topics as nationalism or colonial slavery."[33]

It is true that Coco desires to relate herself to the West, be it the Western philosophies garnishing the beginning of each chapter or the physical ecstasy provided by a German businessman. Her life is associated with the foreign: her Chinese lover who lives on money from Spain, German businessman, art film directors and the various commodities she consumes. Yet Coco is not purely "exploited" by the foreign. Instead, she takes advantage of these foreign-related opportunities and turns them into her own favors. She enjoys the consumption of sexual pleasure and foreign commodities. Her relation to the foreign is less of a national focus than a personal fantasy.

Therefore, I would like to approach it from another perspective. I read Coco's treatment of love and desire as a female fantasy. The fact that a stylish urban female is able to embrace both Chinese spiritual love (provided by Tian Tian) and Western physical pleasure (enabled by Mark) is one kind of personal spiritual/physical fulfillment in the global context.[34] Coco's open enjoyment and graphic treatment of sex is not necessarily a resistance to the mainstream. Rather, it is a self-designed imagination, a deliberate show of a cool life philosophy.

I would like to discuss this issue from Coco's attitude towards both materialism and spiritual engagement. On the one hand, Coco enjoys partying, fancy clothes and fun. On the other hand, she also differentiates herself from other material girls by emphasizing that she is a writer. On one occasion, Coco goes to a luxurious hotel to swim in her red bikini. She is stared at by a pair of Japanese men. She becomes furious at the gaze: "Feminism reared its head. What was it that made me seem so like an empty-headed Barbie doll? Those men probably couldn't guess I was a novelist who'd just shut herself in a room for seven days and seven nights."[35] Here comes the paradox. Though Coco enjoys being sexy and attractive, she expects people to admire her as a beauty writer rather than a mere beauty, a female who possesses both an intelligent mind and a pretty appearance. She needs both material enjoyment and intellectual engagement to confirm her identity and feel fulfilled. Though writing, as I discussed before, is a way for Coco to pursue fame and wealth, Coco still regards writing as a way to bridge her soul and mind.[36] Her writing and her Fudan diploma all serve to confirm that she is a literary woman. A beautiful, transgressive writer is more attractive than just a beauty. Being intellectually glamorous, after all, is what the author herself identified with.

The person who appreciates Coco intellectually and understands her spiritually is Tian Tian. Tian Tian is an artist. He secludes himself from the real world in his apartment and in his artistic engagement. His apartment offers a space for Coco to be away from the disturbance of life and focus on her soul-searching writing. Tian Tian talks Coco into quitting her waitress job and focusing on her writing. Though they have a lack of physical intimacy, Coco feels that "(h)is words were a caress that brought me a joy no other man had ever come near doing."[37]

Coco is nevertheless full of energy and ambition. The world for her is like a "ripe fruit just waiting to be eaten."[38] Though she needs Tian Tian's spiritual support, she also knows how to balance artistic seclusion (writing and painting) and material gain. She even helps Tian Tian turn his artistic creations to profit: she urges Tian Tian to draw paintings on underwear and then she sells the underwear to foreign students.

In various interviews and essays on her novels, Wei Hui has said, "I love pretty clothes, expensive perfume, trashy music, light-scented cigarettes, and witty best-sellers."[39] Naturally, it comes no surprise that Wei Hui named her protagonist Coco, a name associated with French fashion. Coco never disguises her desire for such material culture as fashion, bar-hopping night life. From Wei Hui's narrative of Coco's cosmopolitan daily life, readers can see various brand-name commodities: mild-seven cigarettes, CK underwear, Starbucks coffee, Chanel perfume, and so on. The meticulous description of clothes, hairstyles, parties and architecture also gives readers voyeuristic pleasure and escapist fantasies as they peek at what an alternative cosmopolitan lifestyle should be.

A pale and drug-addicted Tian Tian obviously could not keep up with Coco's ambitious appetites in the consumable city. Economically and physically strong, Mark embodies Coco's bodily and material desire. Mark "was a pillar of society, handsome and intelligent with an enviable job."[40] His identity as a German businessman who works in Shanghai implies his economically privileged status. In the libidinal liaison with Mark, Coco is attracted to him physically. She gives herself up to her desire and succumbs to his masculine power. Moreover, Mark brings the German connection into Coco's life. Through Mark, Coco meets German film-makers and reporters who introduce her to the international art community.

Though torn between spiritual love and physical pleasure, Coco nevertheless enjoys both, though with a sense of guilt or shame. She yields to her desire and keeps both men in her life:

> The man I love can't give me sexual satisfaction, and worse, he can't give me a sense of security. He smokes dope, and he's disengaged from the world...Meanwhile, a married man is giving me physical satisfaction but has no impact on my emotions. We use our bodies to interact and rely on them to sense each other's existence. But they're also a protective layer between us, keeping us from connecting mentally.[41]

For Coco,

> Mark's abilities seemed to have been a gift from the gods, whereas Tian Tian was the total opposite. They were like beings from two different universes. Their existences met in inverted images of themselves projected onto my body.[42]

Spiritual/physical fulfillment in a global/local context is nevertheless short-lived. Though Coco sustains an intimate relationship with her Chinese boyfriend and German lover, both male figures eventually disappear from her life. Her Chinese boyfriend dies and the German lover returns home, again turning Coco's world into a female space. The feminized city ends with the ultimate absence of the male characters.

The disappearance of male figures, however, does not mean that men are rejected and excluded from a female-dominated space in Wei Hui's fictional narrative. On the contrary, Wei Hui's female protagonists, in *Shanghai Baby* as well as other pieces, enjoy and consume men. But they do not depend on them. Men always disappear once they have fulfilled their role of being the object of women's exploration and consumption. Therefore, the female space, in Wei Hui's novels, is constructed to highlight and fulfill female desire. Quite symbolically and ironically, for Coco, the momentary illusion of the fulfillment of both spiritual and physical desires is broken once the males disappear. Wei Hui seems to hint at the impossibility of female exploration. Though it is true that women could independently and hedonistically consume both the city and men, female desire would also lose its ground and be short-lived without the participation of men.

The Transnational Consumption of Wei Hui

Though Coco's fantasy is shattered, Wei Hui's transnational fame, mobility, and identity are realized. *Shanghai Baby* was translated into English, Germany, Dutch, and Japanese. It was on the best seller chart in the U.S. and sold very well in Europe.[43] The English version is labeled "the international best-seller."[44] Wei Hui eventually moved to New York. She had fulfilled her ambition of being a stylish, up-to-date writer with international connections.

Does transnational mobility mean that women writers can be empowered by challenging conventions and taking advantage of global market opportunities? An inquiry directed at the transnational consumption of *Shanghai Baby* shows that the femininity and the politics of female writers were represented differently across both cultural and political borders, rendering the female writer into different cultural perspectives.

FIGURE 2. Cover image of *Shanghai Baby* (London: Constable Publishers, 2001).

In the Chinese market, the cover girl is Wei Hui herself. She wears long, straight hair. Her face, which only occupies a small proportion of the page, and her shoulder gradually merge into the color of the book cover. Half of her face is cut off by the book edge and her eyes are cast down.[45] The cover image is blurry, and the feminine representation fits the classic expectation of a demure and reserved Chinese beauty, though the narrative challenges traditional morality and causes the public anxiety.

In the British version, the blurry image of the Chinese cover girl is more pronounced. Her red lips, long black hair, and the naked shoulder highlight an Asian femininity (Figure 2). The American market also sees a more aggressive image. The English copy has a young Chinese woman's face dominating the cover page. In the picture, she looks up and gazes back at readers, not without a hint of seduction. Her eyes, half-open lips, and slightly tangled hair underscore an exotic look.[46]

Determined from different ideological perspectives, the subject of the gaze is different across national and ideological borders. Yet the gaze is the same in the sense that it expects attractive and beautiful images to sell well. The Shanghai baby is looked at and objectified by transnational readers. Her image is adjusted by transnational companies to fit different ideologies and meet various market expectations. Though sexiness and attractiveness can go further once they cross cultural borders, the female writer is still subjected to the ideology of global consumer capitalism.

Shanghai Baby ends differently in the Chinese and English versions. In the last chapter of the original Chinese version, the I-narrator finishes her novel and turns the book manuscript in to the publishers. In this way, readers learn of the completion of the writing and the meta-fiction is concluded. Chinese readers therefore see the playful manipulation of the half-real and half-fake story. The English version, however, stops at Coco's questioning of "who am I" after both the spiritual love and physical pleasures are gone. The absence of the original last chapter renders the story as the narrative of a female journey of self-exploration. What sells in the American market is a (Chinese) female's rebellious challenge to convention and the impossibility of female desire in the particular modern space of China. In this way, the non-Chinese version downplays its original playfulness and puts Wei Hui's writing into a self-consciously political framework.

Wei Hui's hedonistic and libidinal consumption of the city through writing created a controversial sensation in the market, media, and academia. She was projected as a *linglei* writer-cum-star. Nevertheless, the domestic and international media responded to Wei Hui's book differently. In China's media space, various comments and messages were posted across the Internet discussion forums, a relatively less-censored media space. Based on the discussion messages posted on "http://edu.sina.com.cn/2000-05-05/5/33.html," I summarize three types of attitudes towards Wei Hui. Those who condemned Wei Hui accused her of being an exhibitionist, a slave to foreign culture, and a writer with bad taste, and a prostitute. Those who defended Wei Hui claimed that Wei Hui brought to light a woman's desire and feeling, and her attitude was much more sincere and decent than male writers such as Jia Pingwa, the author of *Fei Du* (Faded capital).[47] The third group dismissed *Shanghai Baby* as a mediocre book with an ordinary plot and amateurish technique. It would have passed into oblivion were it not for the participation of the media and the official ban.[48]

The international market, nevertheless, mainly focused on the fact that the book was "banned and burned" because of its sexual content. Some book reviews say *Shanghai Baby* is "China's first authentic sex'n'shopping novel,"[49] "China's little red book of sex and the city."[50] Because the ban was officially issued by the Chinese Communist Party, Wei Hui became a spokeswoman of the new generation, the cultural rebel of China.[51]

As Wei Hui empowered herself and realized her fantasy through writing, she was also consumed in the transnational market, where she was subjected to a mixture of ideologies. Her Chinese playfulness was downplayed and her political perspective in China's context was highlighted. As she put it in the last chapter of the Chinese version of *Shanghai Baobei*, omitted in the English version: "Once the book is done, it is out of my view and my control."[52]

Wei Hui's Symbolic Return

When Wei Hui wrote *Shanghai Baby*, she had not yet been to other countries. Her cosmopolitan and transnational experience was mainly related to the imaginary she gathered locally. With the commercial and sensational success of *Shanghai Baby*, Wei Hui got the chance to travel outside China. After four years of a relatively low-key life in America, Wei Hui came back to the public spotlight again in 2004 with her new book *Marrying Buddha* (Wo de can), a book signaling her return home.[53]

Wei Hui admitted that her new book examines "homecoming."[54] The protagonist of *Marrying Buddha* is also Coco. Coco returns to her roots on three levels. Geographically, after traveling between New York and Shanghai, she returns to her hometown, her birthplace, a quiet, secluded island. Culturally, she identifies with Buddhism, Confucianism, and Taoism. In the bustling, desire-laden metropolises, Coco finds mental peace in Buddhism. In addition to quotes from Western philosophies and pop songs, Wei Hui also quotes lines from Confucius, Laozi, and Zhuangzi at the beginning of each chapter. Ethically, she returns to the role of a mother. When she goes back to her hometown, she finds herself pregnant without knowing who the baby's father might be. A single mother with a fatherless child symbolizes her negotiations with conventions. After being on a transnational journey, her Chinese "spiritual" love is literarily realized in her transnational journey.

Wei Hui is not the first woman writer who has been vocal about female sexuality. May Fourth writer Ding Ling's *Miss Sophia's Diary* features a woman protagonist Sophia who struggles in her triangular relation with a physically attractive Singaporean man and an emotionally dedicated Chinese man. In the early 1990s, Lin Bai and Chen Ran were very audacious in exposing female sexual fantasy and same-sex desire. Wei Hui's contemporaries, such as

Zhao Bo, Wei Wei, and Zhou Jieru, also had elaborated exploration of sexuality. Why was it Wei Hui who disturbed Party officials and made the public uneasy?

What was different about Wei Hui was her self-promotion and public showcasing. Unlike Ding Ling, whose later revolutionary passion was redemptive of her early bourgeois sentiment; or Lin Bai and Chen Ran, who remained relatively low-key in the commercial market, Wei Hui worked with the media and capitalized on the making and selling of "Wei Hui." Her self-fashioning made her a spokesperson for the beauty writer and a code of decadence. She positioned herself as a glamorous writer, demystifying writing as just one of many professions in the city, and also actualized female longing for being accorded a new kind of humanity in the metropolis. Her self-representation in the text and high-profile performance in the market subverted the conventional image of a writer.

The inter-textural reading of Wei Hui and her novels shows that Wei Hui carried out the career plan and lifestyle she had designed in the texts. As Wei Hui presented an unconventional female subjectivity, she was also consumed in different markets as the different object: a decadent female, a cultural rebel and an exotic sex symbol. Her representation of female desire brought to light the issue of "body writing" as well as the gender politics behind the beauty scenario, which I will discuss in the following chapter.

CHAPTER FIVE

Body Writing

A quick glance at the novel titles *Feng ru fei tun* (*Big breasts and wide hips* by Mo Yan), *Zhengjiu rufang* (*Save the breasts* by Bi Shumin), *Leng chun* (*Cold lips* by Zhao Nin) and *Ti Xiang* (*Fragrance of the body* by Zhao Nin) would be enough to perceive the increasingly visible body in literary texts. Body adornment, such as clothes, makeup, etc., and bodily desire, such as female sexuality, are frequently discussed. This focus has given birth to a new generic term, "body writing" (*shenti xiezuo*).

This chapter examines the body writing phenomenon as it was manifested in different cultural and political discourses. Body writing has been closely related to the seventies writers. The making of body writing in China's context is an interesting process. Different social forces were involved in both the construction and the interpretation of body writing. In Hélène Cixous' original theoretical framework, body writing is a political agenda for women to resist the male-centered ideology inscribed in the general meaning systems proposed by psychoanalytic theorists. Without knowing Cixous' ideas, Ge Hongbing first created the term *shenti xiezuo* (body writing) to express an ideal of using subjective experience and intuition to resist a rationality (*li xing*) characterized by social rules.[1] As the market appropriated body writing, however, the term became sexual, voyeuristically charged, and misogynistic. The feminist, intellectual and commercial messages of body writing converged in the body narrative practiced by female writers. For writers, the obsession with the body was related to various factors: social repression, unrealizable fantasy, infatuation with commodities, playful rebellion, and postmodern pleasure-seeking desire enabled by consumer culture in the new global context.

Various kinds of creation, re-creation, appropriation, and interpretation of body writing reflect social responses to the fact that the body, as a formerly private discourse, was brought to the public arena and gained increasingly prominent cultural status. Interestingly, it was the popular reading of the female body that made the concept of body writing well known. In the over-arching dominance of commercialization, body, bodily desire and body consumption were narrated as a fashion with moral concerns. This reading shows how the female body was disciplined/appropriated to fit with a male's understanding/fantasy of women: the same paternalistic traps against which Cixous had initially warned.[2]

Yet, as Cixous said, women should not stop because of patriarchal traps. At least, women did speak, and they did not keep silence about their bodies any more, and from this perspective, body writing itself was a positive act. Moreover, women were active in distributing their images and texts. At the cost of being objectified and morally judged from within the paternalistic framework, she nevertheless transgressed the trap from within. Body writing is therefore a double-edge sword, voicing women's subjectivity but also transporting women into the public gaze.

Body Writing and Hélène Cixous

Helene Cixous commented on female sexuality in "The Laugh of Medusa" in 1976. Cixous regards female private exploration as:

> A world of searching, the elaboration of a knowledge, on the basis of a systematic experimentation with the bodily functions, a passionate and precise interrogation of her erotogeneity. This practice, extraordinarily rich and inventive, in particular as concerns masturbation, is prolonged or accompanied by a production of forms, a veritable aesthetic activity, each stage of rapture inscribing a resonant vision, a composition, something beautiful. Beauty will no longer be forbidden.[3]

Further, Cixous encourages woman to write out her experience:

> I wish that woman should write and proclaim this unique empire so that other women, other unacknowledged sovereigns, might exclaim: I, too, overflow; my desires have invented new desires, my body knows unheard-of songs.[4]

Cixous affirms that any body function, which includes sexual self-exploration, is a positive self-exploration and expression. She encourages women to explore the uniqueness of the woman's body and bodily functions and turn them into textual power.

Cixous' proposal is part of her broader agenda of *écriture féminine*, which aims at confronting male psychoanalytic theory. Feminists such as Lucy Irigaray and Helene Cixous challenge the language and structure of sexuality proposed by psychoanalysts such as Freud and Lacan. According to Cixous, both writing and the female body have been dominated by a phallocentric economy. Patriarchal stereotypes belittle and demonize women, placing them in a culturally marginal space. To speak out in her own voice and resist the phallocentric misrepresentation of females, a woman should write, and write in a way that is not constrained by the male-centered institutions. To achieve this, Cixous proposes body writing: woman returns to her body and writes through the body:

> Write your self. Your body must be heard. Only then will the immense resources of the unconscious spring forth. Our naphtha will spread, throughout the world, without dollars—black or gold—nonassessed values that will change the rules of the old game.[5]

While the female body is involved in her texts and her private life intermingled with her social engagement, namely writing, she is inevitably exposed to various social forces: capitalism, patriarchal judgment and more. The banning of *Shanghai Baby* is a typical example of how social forces restrain female behavior. Female sexuality, after all, is conventionally a private discourse. Cixous is aware of the patriarchal traps that woman might encounter when this private discourse is disclosed to the public. Nevertheless, she urges woman to keep writing in her own voice:

> Write, let no one hold you back, let nothing stop you: not man; not the imbecilic capitalist machinery, in which publishing houses are the crafty, obsequious relayers of imperatives handed down by an economy that works against us and off our backs; and not *yourself*. Smug-faced readers, managing editors, and big bosses don't like the true texts of women—female-sexed texts. That kind scares them.[6]

Cixous warns women about two types of traps: not only could male-dominated readership and capitalism be hostile to woman, but a woman might be her own obstacle if she gives in to outside pressure. The female-sexed text challenges the male-identified readers' concepts of conventional female sexuality and provokes their insecurity and uneasiness. Men would, she warns, inevitably employ social forces to ensure they form part of that desire and therefore can remain in control of female sexuality. Yet she maintains that a woman should not stop writing and speaking because of this entrapment, for however vicious the trap is, at least she will be making her voice heard. In fact, in Cixous' view, femininity, female bodies, and female sexuality are yet to be explored:

> Almost everything is yet to be written by women about femininity: about their sexuality, that is, its infinite and mobile complexity, about their eroticization, sudden turn-

ons of a certain miniscule-immense area of their bodies; not about destiny, but about the adventure of such and such drive, about trips, crossings, trudges, abrupt and gradual awakenings, discoveries of a zone at one time timorous and soon to be forth-right. A woman's body, with its thousand and one thresholds of ardor—once, by smashing yokes and censors, she lets it articulate the profusion of meanings that run through it in every direction—will make the old single-grooved mother tongue rever-berate with more than one language.[7]

What Cixous implies is that the destination is less important than the journey itself. If the destiny, the purpose, the goal and achievement of the writing, re-mains obscure because of the omnipresent oppositional forces designed to keep a women's body under control, at least woman makes an important step in starting the journey of exploration. The adventure itself is positive and meaningful. It makes a difference and breaks into the patriarchal institution with a new language.

The anti-patriarchal rhetoric is very pronounced in the body writing pro-posed by Cixous. Though emerging in the 1970s as a counter-argument to psychoanalysis, her proposal is still important and applicable in understanding the cultural phenomenon of the body narrative in China of the 1990s. As the political and cultural contexts changed, the concept of body writing has been constructed differently in intellectual, popular, and commercial dis-courses. Different interpretations of body exactly reflect the patriarchal en-trapment that Cixous warned about: women's voices are appropriated to fit in the normative framework. Although female writers did speak up in their own voices, and with a clearly feminist urgency, nevertheless their practice of body writing was also colored by postmodern playfulness and commercial sensa-tionalism.

Shenti Xiezuo: Body Writing as an Intellectual Construction

In China, *Shenti xiezuo* (body writing) started as a concept with totally dif-ferent political implications. The body (*shen*) was initially constructed by critics as a way to resist the over-politicized "mind" (*xin*). Ge Hongbing first used the term *Shenti xiezuo* to comment on a new generation of writers (*xinsheng dai zuo-jia*): a group of urban-based writers, such as Zhu Wen, He Dun, Mian Mian, etc., who were born in both the 1960s and the 1970s. In 1996, Ge Hongbing published an essay titled "The era of individual culture and body writers" (*Geti wenhua shidai yu shenti xing zuojia*).[8] In the essay, Ge argues that post Cultural Revolution China has seen an aesthetic change from collectivity and rational-ity to individuality and intuition. Subjective feelings, rather than rational thinking, constitute the primary principle of the new aesthetic. People rely

more on their subjective experience and their direct contact with their surroundings. In other words, they understand the world through their bodies. [9]
Body writing therefore means that people follow their "sense of touching,"
"sense of hearing," feeling or "instinct" (*ben neng*) as theprincipal way of com-
prehending the world around them. It is a way for people to use their senses
to resist the social repression embodied in various rationalities and rules. [10]

Ge's idea of body writing is similar to Nietzsche's concept that the body
can be used to resist the religious construction of the mind/ spiritual-
ity/rationality:

> If you write about the body from the perspective of the soul, you would think that the
> body is only a form, and we have to use our soul to conquer our body...We would
> think the body is dirty...If we use the body to write about the body, we can confront
> our deep feeling of aloneness, melancholy, and fear. We can experience our physical
> impulses. I regard it as our normal being, our natural humanity... The body itself is
> beautiful and has its own morality.[11]

The target of Ge's body writing criticism is the hypocritical collectivity in the
over-politicized literary works of the Maoist and early post-Mao eras. His proposal of body-writing actually refers to the individual as a humanistic subject
and stresses the political importance of the individual and the individual's
experience.

Ge's understanding of body writing was shared by many critics. Xie Youshun offers a historical perspective of the cultural status of the body. He points
out that, in the dichotomy of body/mind, the mind is always the sublime, and
the body is the dirty and the vulgar.[12] In traditional moral teaching, the body
needs to be sacrificed for the fulfillment of virtue. For instance, Mencius encouraged people to attain the sublime goal this way, "I like life, and I also like
righteousness. If I cannot keep the two together, I will let life go, and choose
righteousness."[13] Life, the basic form of the body, is unimportant and should
perish for the sake of the loftier goal of moral virtue. Though the post-
revolutionary 1980s saw the attempt to revive the repressed individual subjectivity, and words like "individual," "self" and "private" gradually entered into
literary discourse, the body was still absent in literary writing.[14]

In fact, as early as the 1980s, avant-garde writers such as Yu Hua and Ma
Yuan started to explore corporality in their writings. Yu Hua's novels, for instance, feature minute descriptions of the procedures of physical disembodi-
ment. In his novella "Xianshi yizhong" (One kind of reality), Yu Hua gives a
nonchalant account of how an accident leads to a bloody family tragedy. A
little boy accidentally drops and kills his baby nephew. For revenge, the
nephew's father kills the boy, and then he himself is killed by the boy's father.

After the boy's father Shangang is executed for the murder, his organs are harvested by the doctors:

> One doctor picks up her scalpel and thrusts it into the hollow just below Shangang's neck. The incision is perfectly straight, drawing a chorus of admiring gasps from other doctors... The chest surgeon has already removed the lungs and is now merrily cutting through Shangang's pulmonary artery and pulmonary vein, followed by the aorta, and finally all the other blood vessels and nerves coming out of the heart. [15]

Then Shangang's chest and abdomen are excavated, and the stomach, liver, and lungs removed. The grotesque images of bloodshed are allegories of violence within the social institutions of families and hospitals. The objective tone is also a linguistic experiment: an attempt to challenge the dominant style of socialist realism. The body here becomes a vehicle for intellectual exploration and cultural reflection. This kind of body with various cultural messages was exactly what the new generation of body writers opposed.

The first visible practice of body writing started with a group of seventies young poets rather than the beauty writers. Poets Shen Haobo, Yin Lichuan and Duo Yu claim that body has been contaminated by the outside influence of culture, tradition, and politics. To restore the alienated body to its true, pure status, poets would have to return to pure corporeality. To exercise their claim, poets inaugurated a non-official poetry journal *Xia ban shen* (the lower part of the body). [16] Corporeality was their focus. Shen Haobo puts it this way:

> The writing of "the lower part of the body" has as its main aim to pursue the presence of corporeality...Too often, people do not acknowledge their corporeality. Instead, they only have a soft "cultural body" ...To return to corporality means to return to the essential, original and, therefore, corporeal experience. [17]

The philosophy of the "lower part of the body" can be seen in the following poem, "Weishenme bu zai shufu yidian" (Why not be more comfortable) by Yin Lichuan:

Ah, up, down, left, right
This is not making love. This is hammering a nail.
Ah, faster, slower, looser and tighter
This is not making love. This is anti-pornography campaigning or tying a shoe lace
Ah, deeper, shallower, softer and harder
This is not making love. It is massaging, writing poems,
    washing heads and massaging feet.
Why not be more comfortable?
Ah, be more comfortable,

Be gentler, be more violent, be more intellectual, be more vulgar
Why not be more comfortable? [18]

In this poem, the poet employs the imagery of various activities, such as "hammering a nail," "anti-pornography campaigning" and "writing poem" etc., to hint that corporeal (sexual) pleasure could be everything and anywhere. Corporeality speaks for life, politics, intellectuals, and daily activity. The world can be comprehended through sexuality. All the activities are to make body more "comfortable" (*shufu*) or sexually satisfied. By focusing on the lower part of the body, the poet rejects any sublime or vulgar meditation. In their philosophy, the body is the body and sex is sex.

Xie Youshun warns that the change from "spiritual utopia" to "corporeal utopia" might go too far, when body writing is exclusively related to sex, desire, and carnal obsession. If the body is dominated by desire, the body would be subordinated to a new round of dictating power. That is why the body needs to be aesthetically re-constructed and a new round of control is needed. What Xie proposes is to combine corporality with the "soul:" a poetic combination of culture, ethics and the body narrative.[19]

In this sense, then, the construction of body writing in China differs from the feminist agenda proposed by Cixous. It does not so much address the gendered meanings of the body as bring into focus the politically repressed individual. That is, it articulates the power of the previously ignored body in resisting what it sees as hypocritical social restrictions. Nevertheless, not every academic critic had positive views on body writing. The commonly heard negative opinions more or less derived from another manifestation of body: the body of popular and commercial discourses.

The Popular Construction of Body and the Market Appropriation of Body Writing

Neither Ge Hongbing nor Xie Youshun explained the fact that it is always the woman's body that is at the center of attention: an issue associated with post-revolution gender politics, commercialization and popular understanding of the body. Though body writing started as a poetic experiment, it was the seventies female writers who publicized this concept through their fiction. This was partially due to the marginalized position of the poetry, as Xie Youshun argues.[20] Moreover, gender politics in the market and media also were involved. Both were closely related to the popular reading of the body and body writing, which understood the body in its attractive physical exhibition and conflated the narrative of the body with the private, the personal, and the sexually charged. Both body and the writing of the body were, unsurprisingly, commercially exploited.

The commercialized female body has been highly visible as the consumer culture of China expands. When Ge Hongming elaborated his "body theory" in 2005, he states that after being eradicated in the revolutionary narrative, the body in contemporary China is associated with desire and consumption.[21] For the most part, under commercial influences, the body is consumption- and commodity-oriented. Brand-name clothes, makeup, perfume, plastic surgery, and diet drugs, all serve to make the perfect, attractive body, which in turn, increases the consumption of commodities. A typical example of the dialectical relation of body and commodity is the making of a "man-made beauty" (renzao meinü). A girl named Hao Lulu spent two years having different plastic surgeries on most parts of her body so that she could have the ideal, perfect look to which she aspired. As her body consumed commodities in order to become perfect, so the body itself was also consumed as a commodity, for after Hao Lulu won the title of being the first man-made beauty in China, she was invited to shoot commercials and TV soap operas, and became a minor celebrity.

The popular reading of body writing was directly associated with the lucrative construction and consumption of the beautiful female body. Though Ge Hongbing emphasizes that his concept of body writing means "using intuition to resist social repression," and that "it has nothing to do with either beauty or sexuality,"[22] as the sensation-seeking and profit-oriented market conveniently appropriated the term body writing, the feminist or intellectual messages gave way to commercial sensationalism. It was the writes' attractive bodies that had been promoted for public consumption of both a woman and her writing. In this way, public attention was diverted from the text to female writers themselves. Body writing became a sexual term, referring to the depiction of the corporeal body, the graphic portrayal of female sexuality, and writers' public display of their attractive, sexualized images.

The popular critique, accordingly, was mostly moral criticism of female writers, rather than of the texts themselves. Most of the essays in magazines, newspapers, and the Internet equated the textual representation of the body and sexuality with the female writer's actual life experience and therefore concluded that the female writer was shameless and loose in selling her privacy. In a book entitled Shi meinü zuojia piping shu, (Criticizing ten beauty writers), the author, with a pen name Ta Ai (He loves), strongly rebukes body writing:

> As her clothes become fewer and fewer her ambition becomes bigger and bigger. She is less and less good at sentences, but better and better at action. She loses the soul of language. All she has is her body.[23]

An ambitious beauty writer does not need to observe life and experience common people's life. All she needs to do is to shut herself in the bathroom and look in the mirror. Shamelessly reflecting her own body is her only way to reflect life.[24]

Ta Ai then concludes that, "Sex is the required course for beauty writers who want fame and wealth."[25]

Both the book title (*pi pan shu*) and his severe language are reminiscent of various big-character posters (*da zi bao*) of the Cultural Revolution. The verbal violence between the lines almost becomes a personal attack on writers. Though the book is not a strict academic evaluation, it nevertheless reflects one kind of mentality: a misogynistic view, which was by no means a minority view.

This popular condemnation of body writing reflects layers of cultural psyche. Textually and sexually aggressive women challenge social conventions. Verbal violence, as embodied in the "*pi pan shu*," reflects a public uneasiness over unruly women who test moral limits. Men accuse her of being a femme fatale so as to put her into the existing moral framework. Body writing, in this frame of reference, is the exposure of women's sexual experience and narcissistic self-indulgence. Both beauty and body writing, understood as morally degrading, shameless, narrow-minded and decadent, become the major framework for the media and market to categorize most of the seventies female writers.

Because of the widely known negative implication of body writing, female writers themselves rejected the term. Wei Hui was quite sharp on this point: "I use my computer to write and some people use their bodies to read."[26] Jiu Dan responded, "What is body writing? Is it sleeping with men, writing it down, and then publishing it by sleeping with another male editor? If so, I tell you: my book is absolutely not body writing. But if body writing refers to experiencing life through your body, and then expressing the most real and genuine stuff through literary creation, then that is what mine is."[27] Mian Mian said, "'Body is not desire or sensory organs. It is a transparent, closer-to-the-body way through which people employ their intuition to understand rationality."[28]

Cixous asserts that "smug-faced readers, managing editors, and big bosses" do not like female-sexed texts.[29] Her statement is true in the sense that men feel insecure about women's open talk on female sexuality in the public sphere. However, in capitalistic societies, the female-sexed text is also commercially packaged and widely marketed. It is through the very collective voyeurism that both body writing and the critique of body writing sell in the market and publishers make profits. The endlessly emerging copies of books written by the Newly-new generation were good examples.

Yan Hong revealed that the publisher selected their best pictures, set up certain public images for them, and changed her novel title from "I heard love comes back" into "Say it, I am your lover."[30] The new title, with the words "lover," "I" and "your," implies a sexually charged male-female liaison. It appears more sensational than the original title. The public image constructed by publishers for marketing the female writers emphasizes that these are sexy women who are part of the vanguard, leading sensational lives.

The commercial promotion of the body and the popular reading of body writing playfully submitted women to the public voyeuristic gaze. Nevertheless, it was through the popular reading of body writing that it continued to hold market share and public attention. Publishers and writers also maintained a delicate love-hate relationship. Publishers liked the commercial sensation this writing brought, though they also feared female sexual power. An Boshun, manager-in-general of Spring Breeze Publishing House, which published Wei Hui's *Shanghai Baby*, for instance, blamed Wei Hui for her excessive "irresponsible" grandstanding in the market.[31] Writers cooperated with publishers and willingly allowed themselves to be packaged. Yet they also accused the publishers of exploiting and distorting their original intention. The cooperation and tension between the two parties reflect the intermingled feminism, intellectualism, commercialism and capitalist manipulation in the making of the body narrative.

Returning to the Body Itself

The increasingly visible female body, to a large extent, indicates the increasing number of women involved in describing female sexuality. Different interpretations of body writing lie in different recognitions of the cultural roles that female sexuality plays. The transgressiveness of the Newly-new generation, in Liu Jianmei's view, is due to the fact that their portrayal of sexuality falls out of the "revolution plus love" model, the usual model with which people are familiar and the "normal" way that people can accept the subject of sex.[32]

According to Liu Jianmei, the treatment of sex and sexuality in Chinese novels of the first part of the twentieth century was set in the parameter of "revolution plus love." In May Fourth writings, love and sexuality are justified in the novels of both male and female writers because of their association with national and revolutionary subjects. In the post-Mao era, male writers such as Zhang Xianliang, Su Tong, Mo Yan and Ge Fei also explored the subject of sex. Though their treatment of sex, sexuality, and erotica first challenged readers' revolutionary morality, they "employ sex as a narrative strategy to deconstruct the meta-narrative of national myth, revolutionary history, and critical realism." [33] Sex is the expression of their detachment from revolutionary ideology, and therefore is still laden with political allegory. [34]

Some born-in-the-60s writers, such as Chen Ran and Lin Bai, explored female sexuality. Their portrayal of sexuality was part of their private approach to recounting female stories. Rejecting the conventional constructions of woman, Chen Ran and Lin Bai turned to the female body to re-think gender and identity politics. [35] The subject of female sexuality in the novels of Lin Bai and Chen Ran is women's radical rejection of patriarchal institutions such as marriage and the family. The body is laden with feminist agendas. As Li Jingze put it, sexuality in the texts of the born-in-the-60s generation is treated as "something deep." [36]

Wei Wei, one of the seventies writers, compared Chen's generation with her own in her short story "Sexual consciousness at different ages" (Yige nianling de xing yishi). [37] She admits that Lin Bai and Chen Ran are passionate and idealistic in exploring the feministic agenda through sexualized female bodies, whereas her generation is more worldly and pragmatic than their zealous predecessors. Wei Wei's story relates the I-narrator's growing concern over sexuality. Born in the 70s, she is a girl who loves writing. She is very calm when she first watches pornography, as she is a "pure" and "simple" girl in her friends' eyes. Since she is so calm and indifferent, she feels uneasy about herself. Also she feels she has to behave like this to protect herself.

Then she finds a solution to her rather distorted passion: she finds her escape in writing, "At the tip of our pens, we date guys and confide to them. We dance, scream, and make all sorts of bizarre movements. We are active and happy." [38] Though she realizes it is not right to trust writing more than life, she cannot stop writing more and more sex-associated stories. Repressed passion changes into zeal for this playful verbal game. The flourishing verbal construction of sex and sexuality is a way to express something she cannot realize in real life, a verbal fantasy to make up for what is lacking, a way of exploring, and an ambiguous revenge on her parents' generation. Wei Wei's story can be read as one explanation of the increasingly visible representation of sexuality.

In the texts of 70s female writers in general, both the revolutionary legacy and gender politics are absent. Sexuality breaks away from various cultural meanings and political agendas and returns to the body itself. It becomes part of everyday events, just one among many urbanite desires. Physical desire replaces "deeper" emotions. As Zhao Bo, another Newly-new generation writer, wrote, "Perhaps sex is only sex, when you want to ... offer yourself to him and also get pleasure from it." [39]

Muzi Mei: Body Writing as a Discursive Practice

Wei Wei's representation of sexuality is actualized on the level of imagination. Writing weighs more than the body, and the imaginary is more important than reality. It is Muzi Mei who turned the imaginary into the real, and geared it more towards the body. She represents another dimension of body writing: hers was based on her experience of reality and publicized first on the web in the form of an online diary. The "realness" of her body writing turns her into both an alien and a consumable object.

Of course, one should take into account the different forms the authors employ to make their claims. Wei Wei's discussion of body indulgence occurs in the context of a fictional novel, whereas Muzi Mei's discussion takes the form of diary entries. While novels are often attempts to describe existing reality in a space made safe for criticism by explicitly declaring the work fictional, and while diary entries that explicitly claim to be mere descriptions of reality may be distorted, intentionally or not, by the motives of the author, it seems more reasonable to grant *prima facie* status to the latter as an account of extant reality. Therefore, I am more inclined to treat Muzi Mei's body writing as a description of present reality since one's initial expectations for the literary forms involved are to treat novels as fiction and diaries as attempt's to describe actual experiences.

Muzi Mei, whose real name is Li Li, was an editor of *City Pictorial* in Guangzhou where she wrote a sex column. In 2003, she published her sex diary in her blog. Her frequent sexual encounters with men both shook the public and stimulated great curiosity, the thousands of people viewing her blog briefly paralyzed the web server.[40]

What stunned and upset the public, first and foremost, was Muzi Mei's casual account of her many sexual partners. "It is already midnight and I have had my dinner. It is better to find a stranger to make love to. Pick up a phone number. Agreement is reached in two sentences. It is faster than fast food," and she is "making post-seventies love."[41] On her diary dated on July 8, 2003, she had a long list of the men she liked. For her, sex is a way to communicate with men and deal with life. "I always think that making love is the fastest way to get to know one another."[42] She dismisses sex as being the same as any other daily activity. She writes, "I often stayed overnight at a man's house just for a comfortable hot shower...That winter, I was the most comfortable girl in my dorm."[43]

Unlike Chen Ran and Lin Bai's cultural and political exploration of the body, Muzi Mei demystified sexuality, treating it as basic physical gratification. Different from Wei Wei's imaginary body indulgence, Muzi Mei wrote her sexuality in diary form. Her sexuality breaks away from cultural restraints and morality. In her diary narrative, the body becomes a legitimate entity to be used in acquiring pleasure. She explains her sexual adventure this way, "For pleasure! Of course, I can also study men. Each man has different contents."[44] She openly announced, "My attitude is: dissolute sexual behavior should be technically and materially manageable. This can ensure that your body is perfect and you have the chance to either regret or to keep on enjoying yourself. If you psychologically regard sex as it is, it is just a need like other behaviors. This is a way to prevent your heart from being broken."[45]

Muzi Mei followed her own philosophy and enjoyed bodily pleasure. Her apolitical approach to the body, nevertheless involves a reversal of conventional power games between men and women. It is a woman who openly mocks and casually consumes men. She keeps records of the men who had affairs with her and sometimes revealed their performance and real names in her diary. She openly teased male journalists who wanted to interview her: "Want to interview me? You must go to bed with me first. How much time I can give you depends on how long you can hold out in bed."[46] At this point, her writing acquires a rather menacing power. It not only brings her private body into public discourse, but also openly challenges men's loyalty and potency. And since some of Muzi Mei's one-night-stand partners are married, socially "decent" people, she playfully mocks the moral and the conventional. Accordingly, some online commentators say that Muzi Mei is more of an enemy to men than women.

In one episode of her diary, Muzi Mei takes the position of an observer and comments on herself:

> Why is Muzi Mei so rampant? She does not exchange sex for love, marriage, or money. She does not seduce men (because that is impossible). Meanwhile, she is responsible: she lets people know who she had had intercourse with. She proposes that women give men more opportunities and that prostitution be abolished.[47]

In this way, Muzi Mei played a role of both a performer and an observer. The liaisons she developed with men went beyond "seduction," the usual role for a femme fatale or a loose woman. In the gender game, she played an active role. As a columnist said, "She is consuming men from a woman's perspective. At this point, she is like a female Che Guevara, very subversive."[48]

Undoubtedly, Muzi Mei was a totally new and alien figure who broke away from conventional morality and gender norms. She explored her body, spoke up about it and wrote it out. She fit in Cixous's agenda of disregarding paternal language and creating her own aesthetic. Nevertheless, the intriguing fact is that Muzi Mei's sensation was publicized on a *blog*. This kind of online diary extended the space of body writing for women and made self-expression more real and possible than before. The technology-enabled diary also drew voyeuristic readings, which turned Muzi Mei's rebellion and liberation into a dramatic fashion and a collective carnival. The playful consumption of Muzi Mei within the paternal framework made her "sexual revolution" a performance art.

In one of many interviews, Muzi Mei asked her readers to read her sex diary as a literary work. However, it was exactly through the diary's non-literariness that Muzi Mei excited the public. The storyline of Muzi Mei's diary was not complicated. It was the realness of her life that made her a widely known figure. Her most attractive selling-point was her frank account of her sexual adventures. The blog, a new technology-enabled medium, denotes the less restrained expression. The diary-form suggests the real. Both made Muzi Mei's adventure more true than literary.

Muzi Mei certainly broke conventions by disclosing her sexuality and writing about her body. She successfully used the web blog and extended body writing into a bigger space and to a larger audience. In this online space, there were no visible editors and publishers. The exposure of body writing was not initially for money either. From this perspective, Muzi Mei's employment of the blog created a new (alternative) way of writing for women to express themselves. This voice was otherwise repressed in conventionally mediated public spaces such as newspapers, magazines, and journals. As it turned out, later several other female figures, such as "Zhuying qingtong" (Bamboo shadow and blue pupil) and "Furong jiejie" (Sister lotus), followed suit and publicized their pictures, notes, or both on the Internet. Their behavior and self-expression, in the conventional sense, seems absurd, ridiculous and corrupt. They would never make it into the public eye if it were not for the new media of the discussion forum and the blog. Thanks to online space, they were able to circulate their journals and become widely known.[49] Though questions of morality and ethics inevitably arose, the blog nevertheless provided a bigger space for women to express an alternative narrative of the body, and therefore played a positive role in female body writing.[50]

However, it was also the "real" nature of the blog and diary that put the reading public into the position of onlookers, gazers and voyeurs, who could click on the link and find out what how wild a woman can be. Body writing, in the form of the diary and the blog, turned Muzi Mei into an object, pandering to the collective voyeuristic desire of seeing the secret and the forbidden. That was how Muzi Mei's alternative writing was popularized. Muzi Mei supplied the image of a femme fatale. She fulfilled people's fantasy of imagining a loose woman having casual sex.

Interestingly, public curiosity about and enthusiasm for reading woman's private writing also made the concept of the blog, the public media, more widely known. The Chinese term "bo ke" (blog), literally "erudite guest," was first introduced to China by two male Internet experts in 2002.[51] Since then, many people have tried to promote a "blog culture" in China. But it was Muzi

Mei and her body writing that made the blog a household word and later a wide-scale practice. This produces an interesting cycle: a woman appropriates a male-initiated space, has her narrative of the body widely read, and breaks through the patriarchal discourse from within, which in turn, promotes a new medium for men.

Coda

Body writing has different cultural manifestations in different social discourses. The original feminist meaning of body writing gave way to various interpretations in China. Intellectually, the body was constructed as a humanistic individual subject resisting the over-politicized mind. On the popular level, the body was related to desire and commodities, commercially appropriated, and morally condemned.

The feminist, intellectual, and commercial readings of body writing were all embodied in the body writing practiced by women writers and poets. Women's self-representation of female sexuality gave new meaning to the female body and challenged the conventional paternal language. Muzi Mei's exploration of a new writing space, namely, the online blog, publicized female narrative and made woman's voice heard. From this perspective, the woman's body writing was quite feminist and path-breaking. Moreover, the body was constructed by the writers as a legitimate entity that could seek its own pleasure, desire, and experience. It returned from its former function as an ideological and cultural carrier. However, it was always the woman's body and body writing that caught people's attention. The woman's body was objectified and became a lucrative commodity in the market. Women's writing was subjected to voyeuristic reading and commercial exploitation. Though Ge Hongbing warned, "'Body writing' can be used in my literary criticism, but not in the newspaper, because there is no professional foundation for a correct understanding,"[52] it was the vulgarized reading of the body that made body writing well known.

The intermingled feminist, intellectual, and commercial messages turned the body and body writing into a postmodern performance, which was best embodied in Muzi Mei's case. Muzi Mei challenged the convention by naturalizing female body desire. She took advantage of the Internet blog and circulated her body narrative. The new space made the body widely known. The blog expanded women's writing and performance space, and it also submitted her to playful consumption. Ironically, it was the voyeuristic interests that popularized the blog as a household concept. Because of her self-fashioned body, postmodern playfulness, business promotion, collective voyeurism, and feminism, the "liberation" that Muzi Mei created was more like fashion and the performing arts, participated in by both the writer and the public.

Body writing in China's context had acquired different interpretations. When female writers made their body narrative heard in the public, they were also colonized or self-colonized to fit patriarchal language. At the same time, their writing had become increasingly involved with other social factors such as the market and the technology. Nevertheless, women did speak up about their bodies, an act which introduced an alternative voice in the public realm. From this perspective, body writing marked a new moment as a social and literary text.

CONCLUSION

This book has examined a "glamorous" literary and cultural moment in China at the turn of 21st century, the emergence of a group of high-profile female writers born in the seventies. I scrutinize the interfaces between fiction, non-fiction, high culture, and low culture. Dubbed as beauty writers or glam-lit writers, their emergence as both writers and pop stars highlighted the deconstruction of the elite literary sphere and incited anxiety over the vulgarization and commercialization of literature and writers. As both social and literary texts, the phenomenon of beauty writing brought to light a series of literary, cultural, and social issues at an important moment of institutional and ideological transformation, a time when China was ever more actively participating in the global market economy.

After decades of beauty fear, connected with residual effects of feudalism and imperialism, the beauty writers emerged and engaged in a (self) reconstruction of beautiful femininity through a reconfiguration of writing in the post-revolution era. Following the vanguard footstep of the women writers of the previous generation such as Xu Bin, Lin Bai, and Chen Ran, who initiated active female self-exploration, seventies female writers launched a new wave of self-representation of the body, femininity and bodily desire. Their writing challenged conventions and created new literary and aesthetic norms. It turned out that most of these new norms, which were initially provocative, such as the tell-all-style stories and the glamorous packaging of writers, became naturalized and mainstreamed as time went on. From this perspective, female writers contributed to changing the way society views and accepts literature, and they played a transitional role in the development of Chinese literature.

As commercialization and consumerism have become the prevailing powers in cultural production, the self-fashioning female writers inevitably became highly visible objects of desire. Their images, bodies, and visual representations were consumed along with their texts. Their self-representation of female sexuality, their alternative lifestyles, their collaboration with for-profit industries and their incorporation of all of these aspects in their writing made them morally and culturally ambiguous figures. Nevertheless, they spoke up within a male-dominated power structure. Crossing the borderline between the elite and the vulgar, they pushed the female self-narrative of femininity, body, and desire into a new perspective.

The Consumption of Male Body

As the culture market actively explores the exchange value of feminine beauty (*nanse*) literarily "male beauty, sex/love," has also become an increasingly popular commodity. TV entertainment programs such as *Meiren guan* ("Beauty Pass" by Star TV) and *Juedui nanren* ("Absolute Men" by the Hunan Economy Channel) asked a female audience to evaluate physically and culturally beautiful male candidates. At the end of 2004, a controversial "Mr. China" pageant was held in Beijing. In these events, men were brought under the direct scrutiny of a female audience. Male candidates showed their bodies and answered questions, much like women in a beauty pageant. Women became the onlookers, actively consuming male images, and men the object to be gazed upon. The conventional male subject vs. female object relation was inverted. In the *Meiren guan* program, men had to go through a "pass" of women: they were questioned and judged by women. To the approving screams of the female audience, the rejected ones were kicked into a small pond. One could read this as a metaphor of women's symbolic control over men.

A closer look at the consumption of *nanse* reveals a more nuanced scenario. Even in the *nanse* program such as the "Beauty Pass," a feminine *meiren* was employed to promote the event. In 2003, the TV soap opera *Liuxing hua-yuan* (Meteor Garden), featuring "F4" (four "flower-like" young men), was a market hit. The four "flower-like" young men, with their slim figures, long hair, smooth skin, thin lips and stylish clothes, suggested a sexually and physically ambiguous image with both feminine and masculine characteristics. By comparing (young) men to flowers and packaging them as flowery male beauties, the market feminized male figures. It appears that the exotic feminized presentation of the male figures was crucial to the high demand.

The flower-like men did not constitute a threat to the male mainstream, and also pleased the female public, who experienced the role of active onlookers. In this way, the market profited from men, the *nanse*, and also kept conventional manhood intact: it was the feminized young men who were subjected to market manipulation. By feminizing male figures, the market and the media put men into a familiar female position. They presented an illusion of women's empowerment without offending the patriarchal mainstream. What was reinforced subconsciously was actually the "female-object" ideology.

Certainly, there are other types of masculinity in the media represented by actors, athletes and singers. They project various images such as success, power, wealth, courage, assertiveness, determination, and machismo. These male figures, such as basketball player Yao Ming, are admired and worshipped, as the society esteems the cultural traits attached to them. The flower-like men, however, are noted mainly for their feminine characteristics.

The (self) feminization of men is not only seen in the entertainment market, but also in writing. As early as the mid-1980s, Tian Yanning and Tan Li, two male writers in a small Sichuan town, disguised themselves in a figure of an exotic woman from Hong Kong: Xue Mili. Being young back in the eighties, they employed this feminine pen name and wrote detective stories. The exotic Hong Kong woman figure Xue Mili legitimizes the fictional construction of corrupted capitalistic lifestyle of casual dating and crime. Their pulp fiction sold very well, and "Xue Mili" was also a household name in the popular market.

Interestingly, the two men were members of the Writers' Association and serious writers of pure literature. The novels they wrote under their real names, such as "Mountain Road of Ox Dealers" (Niufanzi shandao) by Tian Yanning) and "Lan huabao" by Tan Li, have won literary awards at different levels. Only in their female identity did they write vulgar pulp fiction. Despite commercially packaging themselves as an exotic Hong Kong woman writer, they never actually went to Hong Kong. What they constructed in fiction and sold to the market was their pure imagination of a dazzling capitalistic life style. Their self-otherization and self-feminization legitimized their for-profit writing. Their feminized identity conveniently disguised them and marketed them. After all, the image of a woman figure, especially an exotic Hong Kong woman, was marketable and profitable. In this way, Tian and Tan maintained their original privileged male status in the literary mainstream and meanwhile earned profits through self-feminizing. In the pure literature mainstream one found the conventional male intellectuals. In the commercial market one found the "material girl" figures. The double-identity strategy epitomized and reinforced conventional stereotypes of the serious male and playful female. Also because of the double identity strategy, Tian Yanning and Tan Li did not directly sacrifice their male dignity in public, at least so long as their ruse remained undiscovered.

As if to respond to "hooligan" writer Wang Shuo's playful question "how come there is no such term as 'handsome man writer'," the "beautiful male writer" (meinan zuojia) came on the scene in 2003.[1] Ironically, the person who won this title was Ge Hongbing, the accomplished professor at Shanghai University. He was promoted as a good-looking male and given a meinan title as his semi-autobiographical novel, Sha chuang (Bed of sand), was published. Taking advantage of the sensation created by *meinü* writers, the publicity around the *meinan* title had an obvious commercial motive.

As expected, when a mainstream man, with his intellectual status and role as a professor, sold himself directly as a beautiful male, there was stronger critical backlash laced with mockery, contempt, condemnation, and anger. He was regarded as a cultural hooligan, selling out not only his own dignity as a scholar, but also the dignity of all male intellectuals. Zhu Dake, for instance, was quite sharp in his characterization of Ge Hongbing's activities, "A scholar, instead of working on ideas and literature, runs into the street, naked..."[2] Though the *meinan* strategy did achieve the sensation that the publishing house expected, the writer also paid a tremendous intellectual and moral price as he tarnished his status as an intellectual by appeal to the physicality of a male, the *nanse*.[3]

Bed of Sand involves a young professor's entangled relationship with several women and explores topics of youth, life, illness, and death. Though Ge on many occasions defended himself as a serious intellectual, he received more negative than positive comments.   Later, bothered by various criticisms of his *meinan* title, he claimed he had been a victim of commercialization and even planned to sue both critics and the websites that associated him with the vulgarized image of selling bodies.[4] Victim or not, when a mainstream male directly ventured into the beauty mentality and garnered physical attention, he offended the conventional expectation of a mainstream man and a man's proper social image. Whatever Ge's intention was, he ended up with a notorious public reputation and was viewed as a failed intellectual.

The fact that men have garnered commercial success by blatantly exploiting their beauty raises several questions. Does this show the triumph of feminism in a world where women more routinely occupy the position of active onlookers, while men occupy the position of objects? Or, does this simply reinforce the cultural enchantment with commodification and objectification more generally? It appears, on closer inspection, that the paternalistic ideology has survived intact through this *double space* strategy. In the marginal space, as embodied by youngsters or the two male writers who took a feminine pen name, masculinity can be played with and constructed in various forms, and it can be fluid, feminized, and objectified. In the mainstream space, as Ge Hongbing's case suggests, orthodox male dignity was safeguarded. A female beauty writer, though controversial, was accepted and consumed as the playful and stylish cosmopolitan, whereas a male beauty writer was not what the mainstream could tolerate. The public would not accept the feminization of established male figures. Instead, male literary dignity was cautiously guarded, while the initially shocking female literary engagement was in some sense accepted or at least tolerated, while from a broader perspective it can be seen to have been encouraged and manipulated to achieve commercial ends.

The "Maturing" of Beauty

Beauty is a time-sensitive conception. As a fashion, it cannot remain stagnant, since the market is always pursuing new sensations. Luo Yijia realized this and predicted that she and her four beautiful pals could probably only stay together for a couple of years.[5] As more and more beauties came on the scene projecting a hyper-sweet feminine look, people grew tired of this fad. In 2005, "The voice of super girls" (*chaoji nüsheng*), an American Idol type of entertainment program, was aired by Hunan Satellite TV. Besides the on-the-spot judges, the program also invited audiences to cast their votes for their favorite "super girl" through cell phones and the Internet. Li Yuchun was voted the champion. Her tomboy look, short hair, and boyish manner were a clear subversion of the type of feminine beauty typically portrayed in the media. Given the fact that Li was selected by a majority of the popular votes, her emergence in the public arena suggests shifts in the measures of femininity and beauty, and tracks changes in popular taste. This shift also took place in the popular taste for female writers. After all, just as the sensation-seeking market and the media need new images and voices, so does the literary forum, as writings have been closely related to the market.

Shi Zhanjun, one of the three editors who started and promoted the post-seventies category, published an essay entitled "Gaobie xinsheng dai" (Farewell, new-born generation).[6] He argues that the writing style and narrative content of the new-born generation became increasingly rigid and stereotyped as the "used-to-be-young" generation grew into middle age. Shi claimed they are disappearing from the vanguard of literary writing because their individualized style has become a tired cliché and has lost its initial energy.

This was representative of the attitude and behavior of mainstream male intellectuals. At first, they actively cheered the new voice of female writers; but when these writers became a hit, they denounced them because their subsequent development had passed out of their control. It appears that the men were supportive of the phenomenon and development of beauty writers as long as these male writers could occupy a paternalistic position. Whether one says farewell or not, beauty writers, after creating a stunning sensation, have gradually faded from view in the dominant media. Besides waning interest, many factors were involved in the low-key images of these female writers.

First, "beautiful" packaging has become mainstreamed in the market and the media. A once "cool" style has become the norm. Instead of totally disappearing, beauty became so hyper-visible that it no longer stood out. Beautiful images of women writers are everywhere and therefore no longer unusual, eye-catching, or shocking. The commercial promotion of young female writers has become a widely acknowledged practice, and the commercialization of writing in general has been legitimized in the culture market. This explains why the public was not overly perturbed by the more rebellious and playful youngsters born in the eighties, such as Chun Shu and Guo Jinming, when they staged their literary performance. After the Muzi Mei incident, blogging has been adopted by an increasing number of people as a common mode of expression. Women's active expansion into the public sphere through speaking in cyberspace has been gradually accepted by many people. The only irony is that literature lost its commercial appeal decades after it lost its intellectual appeal.

The second reason is related to the writers themselves. As I argued, female writers emerged as an alternative voice in the literary forum. Their mixed identity as both writers and pop stars, and their textual representation of the new urban youth, body, and desire actualized the personal/national fantasy of the pursuit of wealth and the establishment of a global identity. It also provided a vehicle for both writers and readers to participate in the imaginary construction of a new global citizen in China. Once the image they constructed textually became the everyday urban reality, they started to return to their cultural roots or began to identify with the conventional mainstream.

After gaining the opportunity to stay in the U.S. for years, Wei Hui culturally returned home in her new book *Marrying Buddha*. Mian Mian recovered from her illness, moved to her home, and promoted a more rational and healthy lifestyle. Despite her current part-time job as a nightlife promoter, she found herself staying at home more often than before.[7] Zhou Jieru traveled to the U.S. and became a mother. Anni Baobei switched to regular print media. Muzi Mei obtained a regular position in a mainstream industry, though she still writes her controversial blog. Marginal youth, problem girls, and rebellious youngsters merged into the cultural majority or the comfortable mainstream. As the imagined global mobility and fame was achieved, writers also broke away from their initial obsession with materialism and self.

At the end of 2004, Wei Wei won the Lu Xun Literary Award, one of the most prestigious literary awards given to brilliant, outstanding novelists in China, with her novella "Old Big Zheng's Woman" (Da Lao Zheng de nüren). This was the first time that a post-seventies writer was acknowledged by the literary mainstream. Both the literary critics and Wei Wei were very excited. Critics regarded it as a work in which "a contemporary Chinese novella pays tribute to tradition."[8] Wei Wei also expressed her opinion that the seventies writers are moving towards a more serious way of writing. She said, "The attention and concerns of this group is turning away from commercial packaging and promotion to writing itself."[9] Wei Wei's award was taken as a milestone for the seventies writers, who have actively sought status in the literary mainstream.

"Old Big Zheng's Woman" is drastically different from most of the novellas of Wei Wei's female contemporaries. The story is set in a small town in the early 1980s, when economic reform and opening-up had just gotten underway. It depicts how these changes affected the quiet life of ordinary people such as Old Big Zheng and his woman. Old Big Zheng is a sojourner who makes a modest living buying and selling cheap items. A village woman sells herself to him for money, yet gets along very well with his family. The "buy and sell" relationship brings them together, and both of them love and enjoy it.

Wei Wei's novella reminds readers of Shen Congwen's account of the special customs of Hunan, focusing on seemingly immoral yet human moments.[10] Instead of depicting the fashionable, dazzling cosmopolitan life, the story returns to a quiet small town. Instead of focusing on young, stylish urbanites, Wei Wei went back to the ordinary small-town people with their own philosophy of survival in changing times. Fashionable images, such as clubs and shopping malls are absent. Instead, readers come across familiar things such as the small yard of the residence compound, quiet lanes, and daily gossip. Instead of remaining self-absorbed with her own experience, Wei Wei devoted her attention to everyday life of ordinary people. As it turns out, this literary style won high acclaim from the mainstream.

Wei Wei's case raises once again the rivalry of the traditional versus the modern, and the urban versus the rural. This issue has been discussed since the May Fourth period and continues to fuel debates over China's cultural identity in the age of globalization. While May Fourth writers viewed the countryside as idyllic but also backward, socialist writers recognized the rural as the revolutionary source. Meanwhile, root-searching writers in the post-Mao era sought cultural identity in the remote regions. Subsequently, seventies writers and many other urban fiction writers supplied a new imaginary to accompany the urban frenzy of the 1990s. This played a significant role of constructing a new ideal for China. Against this background, Wei Wei received literary recognition by identifying with the charm of the small town. Her homage to the significant role of the tradition earned her recognition from the literary mainstream and initiated another round of competition in the ongoing battle of cultural authenticity.

As we can see, both the external social practices and writers themselves have contributed to the decreasing visibility of the seventies female writers as a glamorous group. While a sensation-obsessed market looked for the new and the provocative, male critics tended to look for more substantial works and literary accomplishment. Among writers themselves, many like Wei Hui, Mian Mian, and Zhou Jieru returned to their cultural roots by negotiating with the traditional values. Some figures, such as Wei Wei, changed their writing style to identify with the literary mainstream. Meanwhile, the new practices, such as commercial promotion, which were endorsed by this group of writers, became more widely accepted and adopted by the public. As female writers and the conventional mainstream assimilated each other, the shock value, previously associated with these writers and their work, dissipated.

Mainstreamed, transformed or (self) exiled, the former beauty writers have gradually fallen out of the public eye. Nonetheless, it was their timely emergence at the turn of the century that introduced alternative literary voices and painted different visions just at a point when the old aesthetic, moral, and literary discourses were crumbling. The interrelation of writers, readers, media and publishing houses, as well as the interconnection of writings with globalization, capitalism, feminism, the Internet, and the market, were organized around focal points of both mainstream status and market value. Though the sensational moment of seventies writers has been dismissed, the impact of the writers, the uniqueness of the phenomenon, and the confluence of circumstances that led to the phenomenon deserve to be studied. I have shown in my book the relation of the seventies writers to the important cultural events, such as alternative writing, body narrative, cyberspace politics and female self-representation, at the turn of the 21st century. The moment of seventies female writers not only reflected the transformation of literature and culture, but also the change of the society.

NOTES

Introduction

[1] My personal interview with Wang Yuan on July 7, 2004. In this book, unless otherwise noted, all the translations are mine.

[2] In my book, I will use "seventies/70s female writers" or "post-seventies female writers" to address female writers born in the 70s.

[3] Shi Anbin, A Comparative Approach to Redefining Chinese-ness in the Era of Globalization (Lewiston: Mellen Press, 2003),133.

[4] Some critics, such as Ge Hongbing, categorized some seventies writers into the "new generation." See Ge Hongbing, Zhengwu de shixue (Poetics at noon), (Shanghai: Shanghai renming chubanshe, 2001).

[5] "Pure Literature" (chun wenxue) generally refers to the non-commercial novels that engaged in intensive intellectual and cultural exploration of life, arts, and humanities.

[6] Li An, "Congshu 'Qishi niandai hou'" (Reshape "the post-seventies generation"), Furong (Hibiscus) 4, (1999), 8–9.

[7] Wei Hui called herself meinü and zuojia. See Zuojia (Writer) (July 1998): inside front cover.

[8] The blurring boundary of literary writing and pop ficition already started before the beauty writers burst onto the PRC literary scene. "Wang Shuo phenomenon" and his "hooligan literature" is an example. I will elaborate on the changing concept of high culture/low culture in Chapter Four.

[9] See Mian Mian, "Tang (Candy)," Shouhuo (harvest) 1, (2000): 153–208.

[10] Zhongguo xiaoshuo wushi qiang bianweihui (editing committee of "the fifty most important Chinese novels"), "Chongfan qinli de xiaoshuo xianchang—Zhongguo xiaoshuo wushi qiang" (Return to personally experienced scenes of novels: fifty important Chinese novels), in Can Yue, Canglao de Fuyun (Old cloud) (Changchun: Shidai wenyi chubanshe, 2001), 1–4. The committee members are Xie Mian, Wang Mian, Hong Zicheng, Meng Fanhua, Chen Xiaoming and Li Jiefei.

[11] John Berger, Ways of Seeing (New York: Viking Press, 1973).

[12] Simone de Beauvoir, The Second Sex, trans. H. M Parshley (New York: Alfred A. Knopf, 1953): xvi.

[13] Ibid.

96

14   Sandra Lee Bartky, "Narcissism, Femininity and Alienation," *Social Theory and Practice* 8, (Summer 1982): 137–138.

15   Naomi Wolf, *The Beauty Myth: How Images of Beauty Are Used against Women* (New York: W. Morrow, 1991), 12.

16   Ibid.

17   Efrat Tseëlon, *The Masque of Femininity: the Presentation of Woman in Everyday Life* (London: Sage Publications, 1995), 68–69.

18   Ibid., 74.

19   *Zuojia* (July 1998): inside front cover.

20   Wei Hui, "Wo haixiang zenme ne" (What else do I want), *Zuojia* (July 1998): 25.

21   Li Jingze regarded the whole beauty writer phenomena as the degradation of women's status in general when he was interviewed by me on July 29, 2004.

22   Qiu Huadong, "Xin meiren" (New beauty), in *Yaogun Beijing* (Rock'n'Roll in Beijing), (Beijing: Zhongguo Wenlian chunban gongsi, 1998), 371–382.

23   I summarized various comments from the online special column available at http://www.booker.com.cn/gb/paper54/1/class005400034/hwz103319.htm.

24   Ellen Zetzel Lambert, *The Face of Love: Feminism and the Beauty Question* (Boston: Beacon Press, 1995), 16.

25   Ibid., 17.

26   For detailed arguments on how the traditional feminine appearance is associated with identities, see Rebecca Walker, *To be Real: Telling the Truth and Changing the Face of Feminism* (New York: Anchor Books, 1995). For more discussions on third-wave feminism, see Leslie Heywood & Jennifer Drake, ed. *Third Wave Agenda: Being Feminist, Doing Feminism* (Minneapolis: University of Minnesota Press, 1997).

27   Leslie Heywood & Jennifer Drake, 3.

28   Jennifer Baumgardner & Amy Richards, "The Number One Question About Feminism," *Feminist Studies* 29, no. 2 (summer 2003): 450.

29   Mayfair Yang used "gender erasure" to address the Cultural Revolution. See Mayfair Yang, "From Gender Erasure to Gender Difference: State Feminism, Consumer Sexuality and Women's Public Sphere in China," in *Spaces of Their Own*, ed. Mayfair Yang (Minneapolis: University of Minnesota Press, 1999), 35–67.

30   See Wei Wei, "Chong xie chengyu gushi: dui xiaoshuo de yidian lixiang" (Re-writing idiom stories: A little idealism for novels), *Furong*, no. 4 (1999): 38.

31   Ibid.

32   My personal interview with Li Jingze on July 29, 2004.

33   Greene, Gayale, *Changing the Story: Feminist Fiction and the Tradition* (Bloomington: Indiana University Press), 1991.

34   Liang Qichao "Lun xiaoshuo yu qunzhizhi gunaxi" in *Wan Qing wenxue congchao: xiaoshuo xiqu yanjiu juan* (Anthology of late Qing literature: research materials on fiction and drama), ed. A Ying (Beijing 1960), 39, quoted in Shu-ying Tsau, "The Rise of 'New Fiction,'" in *The Chinese Novel at the Turn of the Century*, ed. Dolezelová-Velingerová, Milena (Toronto: University of Toronto Press, 1980), 28.

35   Wei Hui, "Wo haixiang zenme ne?" *Zuojia*: 25.

36   Lori Saint-Martin, "Sexuality and Textuality Entwined: Sexual Proclamations in Women's Confessional Fiction in Québec," in *Confessional Politics: Women's Sexual Self-Representations in Life Writing and Popular media*, ed., Irene Gammel (Carbondale: Southern Illinois University Press, 1999), 28–46.

37   Irene Gammel, ed. *Confessional Politics: Women's Sexual Self-Representations in Life Writing and Popular Media*.

38   Irene Gammel, "Introduction," in *Confessional Politics: Women's Sexual Self-Representations in Life Writing and Popular Media*, 1–10.

39   Ibid.

40   Lori Saint-Martin, 28–46.

41   See Cai Zhizhong, *Cai Zhizhong gudian Manhua* (Cai Zhizhong's classical cartoon) (Beijing: Shenghuo Dushu Xinzhi Sanlian shudian, 2001); *Laozhao pian* series (Old pictures) were published by Shandong huabao chubanshe. From 1998 on, Shandong Pictorial Publishing House published more than twenty episodes. Chen Danyan's "Shanghai memoir"series were published by Zuojia chubanshe.

42   Yang Xiaoyan, "Huashuo dutu shidai–Li Tuo, Liu He zhuanfang" (Talks on image-reading era–interview Li Tuo and Liu He), 30 May 2005, http://www.cul-studies.com/community/lituo/200505/1995.html (accessed November 10, 2005).

43   Roland Barthes, "Ornamental Cookery," trans. in Annette Lavers, *Mythologies* (New York: Hill & Wang, 1972), 78–80, quoted in Ellen MaCracken, *Decoding Women's Magazines: From Mademoiselle to Ms* (New York: St. Martin's Press, 1993), 1.

44   Shao Yanjun, "*Meinü wenxue*" *xianxiang yanjiu: cong* "*70 hou*" *dao* "*80 hou*" (Research on the "beauty literature" phenomenon: from "post-seventies" to "post-eighties") (Guiling: Guangxi shifan daxue chubanshe, 2005).

45   Ta Ai, *Shi meinü zuojia pipanshu* (Criticizing ten beauty writers) (Beijing: Hualing chubanshe, 2005).

Chapter One
From Invisibility to Hyper-Visibility: Constructing Femininity in the Media and Literary Space

1   For detailed elaboration on "glocal," see Roland Robertson, "Glocalization: Time-Space and homogeneity-heterogeneity," in *Global Modernities*, ed. Mike Featherstone, Scott Lash and Roland Robertson (London: Sage, 1995), 25–44.

2   *Zuojia*, originally a literary journal, was changed into a magazine and renamed *Zuojia zazhi* (Writer magazine) in 2000. The fate of the magazine itself is an interesting example of how the elites adjusted to the popular taste at the turn of the century, a point that I will elucidate in Chapter Four.

3   Mao Zedong, "Militia women," in *The Poems of Mao Tse-tung*, trans. Willis Barnstone and Ko Ching-po (New York: Harper & Row, 1972), 99. Mao wrote the poem in 1961.

4   Vanda Burstyn, "Masculine Domination and the State." Cited in Robin Wood, "Images and Women," in *Issues in Feminist Film Criticism*, ed. Patricia Erens (Bloomington and Indianapolis: Indiana University Press, 1990), 337–352.

[5] Li Xiaojiang, "With What Discourse Do We Reflect on Chinese Women? Thoughts on Transnational Feminism in China," in *Spaces of Their Own: Women's Public Sphere in Transnational China*, ed. Mayfair Mei-Hui Yang (Minneapolis: University of Minnesota Press, 1999), 261–277. Li is a famous scholar in women's studies in China, but she refuses to be recognized as a "feminist." See Li Xiaojiang, *Guanyu nuren de dawen* (Answers about women) (Nanjing: Jangsu renming chubanshe, 1997), 58.

[6] Mayfair Yang, "From Gender Erasure to Gender Difference: State Feminism, Consumer Sexuality and Women's Public Sphere in China."

[7] It is argued that men were also "castrated" in the Maoist era. Both men and women were tamed by the CCP to be obedient citizens. See Mayfair Yang, 35–67.

[8] Dai Jinhua, "Invisible Women: Contemporary Chinese Cinema and Women's Film." *Positions* 3.1 (1995):254–80. Hua Mulan is a legendary woman warrior who masquerades as a man so that she can substitute for her aged father and fight in the army.

[9] Chen Xiaomei, *Acting the Right Part: Political Theater and Popular Drama in Contemporary China* (Honolulu: University of Hawai'i Press, 2002), 36–37.

[10] Ibid.

[11] Zhang Xinxin, "How Did I Miss You?" in *One Half of the Sky: Stories from Contemporary Women Writers of China*, trans. R.A. Roberts and Angela Knox (London: Heinneman, 1987), 92–124.

[12] Ibid., 92.

[13] Ibid., 97.

[14] Ibid., 101.

[15] Ibid., 115.

[16] Ibid., 104.

[17] In fact the discussion of femininity in *Women of China* began in the late 1970s, and reached its first peak in the mid-1980s in the broad social context of cultural reflection on Chinese tradition and modernization. The discussion in the early 1990s, initiated by a reader's letter in August 1991, started to involve feminist perspectives on gender roles. See *Women of China* issued between August and December in 1991.

[18] This set of ads ran for many issues. Mine is taken from the back cover of the December issue of 1994.

[19] Pets were the symbol of a well-off lifestyle in China in early 1990s, as they were expensive to obtain and keep. I will discuss the notion of "middle class" in China in Chapter three.

[20] Huang Shuqin, "A Conversation with Huang Shuqin," *Position* 3 (Winter 1995), 790–805. Huang Shuqin is a famous Chinese film director.

[21] Zong Renfa, Shi Zhanjun and Li Jingze, "Guanyu 'qishi niandai ren' de duihua."

[22] Megan Ferry's employment of "paratext" gave me the inspiration to study the 70s writers. See Megan Ferry, "Marketing Chinese Women Writers in the 1990s, or the Politics of Self-Fashioning," *Journal of Contemporary China* 12, no. 37 (November 2003), 655–675.

23 Gerard Genette, "Introduction to the Paratext," *New Literary History* 22, no. 2 (Spring 1991): 261–272. Also see Gérard Genette, *Paratexts: Thresholds of Interpretation* (Cambridge: Cambridge University Press, 1997).

24 My personal interview with Li Jingze on July 29, 2004.

25 Xing Xiaoqun, "Yipi nianqing nü zuojia zanlu toujiao" (A group of young female writers stand out), *Zuojia* (July 1998): back cover.

26 *Zuojia*, inside front cover.

27 Ibid., back inside cover.

28 Ibid., 26.

29 Ibid., 53.

30 Ibid., inside front cover.

31 Ibid., 25. In this issue, not all the writers present themselves as the symbol of new metropolitan style. For instance, some of Jin Renshun and Dai Lai's pictures are taken in the natural scenery.

32 Ibid., 38

33 Ibid., 86.

34 My interview with Li Jingze.

35 "Mian Mian: Jiejin wuxian touming de hongse," (Mian Mian: getting closer to the transparent red," http://www.dragonsource.com/tuijian/mianmian.htm (accessed May 27, 2005).

36 Meng Jinwei, "Shangye baozhuang cuisheng 'meinü zuojia'" (Commercial packaging produces "beauty writers"), http://www.booker.com.cn /gb/paper54 /1/class005400034/hwz103319.htm (accessed June 23, 2003).

37 The "ten Internet beauty writers" were Wei Hui, Mian Mian, Shang Ailan, Hei Keke, Zhou Jieru, Anni Baobei, Shuijin Zhulian, Nan Chen, Wang Maomao and Zhong Kun. Wang Xiaoshan, See "Shi da wangluo meinü zuojia bang," (Ten Internet beauty writers chart), 19 December 2000, http:// culture.163.com/edit/001219/001219_44308.html (accessed June 23, 2003).

38 Wen Rumin, "Jin ershi nian lai Zhang Ailing zai neidi de jieshoushi" (How Zhang Ailing has been read in the recent twenty years). See "Zhang Ailing: cainü haishi meinü? (Zhang Ailing: Beauty or Literary Woman), 1 November 2000, http://culture.163.com/edit/001101/001101_42778.html (accessed June 23, 2003).

39 Li Jingze, "Bei zhebi de qishi niandai ren" (The hidden sventies generation), *Nanfang wentan* (Southern literary forum), no. 4 (2000): 49–51.

40 Li An, "Congshu 'Qishi niandai hou'" (Reshape the post-seventieth), *Furong* (Hibiscus) 4, (1999): 8–9.

Chapter Two
The Changing Faces of Ephemeral Youth: A Reading of Mian Mian

1 Mian Mian, *Candy*, trans., Andrea Lingenfelter (Boston: Little, Brown. 2003).

2 "'Caoyang nianhua' bei Taiwan meiti lieru Zhongguo shi da qingchun xiaoshuo" ("Life like grass" is listed as one of the ten youth novels by Taiwan media), 22

November 2003, http://book.sina.com.cn/news/c/2003-11-22/3/26128.shtml (accessed October 4, 2004). Other "youth novels" of Mainland China include Shi Kang's *Huanghuang youyou* (Shaky), Chun Shu's *Beijing wawa* (Beijing doll), Sun Rui's *Cao yang nianhua* (Life like grass).

3   Li Dazhao, "Spring," trans. Claudia Pozzana, *Positions* 3 (Fall 1995), 306–327.

4   For details, see Tang Xiaobin, *Chinese Modern: The Heroic and the Quotidian* (Durham, NC.: Duke University Press, 2000).

5   Wang Meng, "Qingchun wansui," *Wang Meng Xuanji* (Selected works of Wang Meng), (Tianjin: Baihua wenyi chubanshe, 1984), 360. Wang Meng's *Long Live, Youth* was written between 1953 and 1956. Yet it was not officially published until after the Cultural Revolution.

6   Ru Meng, "Mian Mian: wo bushi meinü bu xiang zuojia" (Mian Mian: I am neither a beauty nor a writer), *Tequ qingnian bao*, 26 July 2002, http://www.step.com.cn/ tqqn/20020726/gb/tqqn%5E178%5E%5ETf001.htm (accessed November 11, 2004).

7   Wei Wei and Zhu Wenying, "Xiezuo, yinxiang he neixin huodong," (Writing, impression and mental activity), *Zuojia zazhi* (Writer magazine) 4, 2003, http://www.writermagazine.com/2003/4/xie.htm (accessed October 6, 2004).

8   "Writers Born in the 1970s Stimulate Debate," *China Daily*, 20 October 2004, http://www.chinadaily.com.cn/english/doc/2004-10/20/content_384079.htm (accessed October 24, 2004).

9   Wu Liang, "Zhe yidai ren de shenghuo he xiezuo" (Life and writing of this generation), *Xiaoshuo jie* (Fiction world) 2, (1997): 180–182.

10   Ge Hongbing, *Zhengwu de shixue* (Poetics at noon), (Shanghai: Shanghai renmin chubanshe, 2001), 224.

11   Wei Wei and Zhu Wenying, "Xiezuo, yinxiang he neixin huodong."

12   Ibid.

13   Ibid.

14   Mian Mian was a rock'n'roll lover. She has worked as DJ and music promoter. She claimed that she always wore an earphone to write. See "Yong pifu xiezuo yong shenti jianyue nanren" (Using my body to inspect men and my skin to write), 13 October 1999, http://users.cgiforme.com/leoxl/messages/84.html (accessed November 14, 2004).

15   Mian Mian, *Candy*, 213.

16   Zhang Lin, "'Xiandaihua' yujing zhong de 90 niandai wenxue zhuanxin" (The transformation of literature of the 1990s in the discourse of "modernity"), *Ershi yi shiji* (21st century), no. 21 (December 2003), 31 December 2003, http://www.usc.cuhk.edu.hk /wk_wzdetails.asp?id=2823 (accessed December 1, 2005).

17   Mian Mian, *Candy*, 209.

18   Ibid., 270.

19   Ibid., 50.

20   This translation is from Megan M. Ferry. See Megan M. Ferry, "Marketing Chinese Women Writers in the 1990s, or the Politics of Self-Fashioning," *Journal of Contemporary China* 12, no. 37 (November 2003), 655–675. Her translation is more accurate in expressing what Mian Mian means in her Chinese text than Lingenfelter's.

21 The story on Tan Tan has been omitted in the English translation.

22 Mian Mian, *Candy*, 128.

23 Mian Mian, "Yige bingren" (One patient), *Furong* (Hibiscus) 4, (1999), 34–36. This story has been included in *Candy* as one chapter.

24 Mian Mian, *Shejiao wu* (Social dance) (Guangzhou: Xin shiji chubanshe, 2002).

25 Susan Sontag, *Illness as Metaphor and AIDS and Its Metaphors* (London: Penguin, 1991).

26 Mian Mian, *Candy*, 129.

27 Ibid., 184.

28 Ibid., 171.

29 Ibid., 184.

30 Michel Foucault, *Language, Counter-Memory and Practice: Selected Essays and Interviews*, trans. Donald F. Bouchard and Sherry Simon (Ithaca: Cornell University Press, 1980): 50–51.

31 "Mian Mian reaches maturity with 'Panda Sex'" *China Daily*, 1 March 2005, http://www.chinadaily.com.cn/english/doc/2005–03/01/content_420714.htm (accessed December 25, 2005).

32 "Mian Mian: jiejin wuxian touming de hongse" (Mian Mian: getting close to the endlessly transparent red), http://www.dragonsource.com/tuijian/ mianmian.htm (accessed November 14, 2004).

33 Mian Mian, "Zhe yichang 'meinü zuojia' de naoju" (The farce of "beauty writers"), http://news.xinhuanet.com/book/2003-03/12/content_773258.htm (accessed December 10, 2004).

34 Zhang Zhe, "Xuezhe wei meinü zuojia 'haomai'" (Scholars feel the "pulse" of beauty writers), http://news.xinhuanet.com/book/2003–03/12/content_773258.htm (accessed December 10, 2004).

35 Wei Hui and Mian Mian had a long-term grudge. Mian Mian accused Wei Hui of plagiarizing her novels. Wei Hui denied it and openly showed her contempt for Mian Mian's high school diploma. Their verbal fight in the media and Internet discussion forum gradually became a personal attack on each other. The media and the public took quite a bit of pleasure in seeing the event. Needless to say, both the fights and the media response were indeed very *bingtai* (morbid).

36 Shao Yanjun has detailed discussion on how the "cruel" has been sold as the "cool" in Mian Mian's case. See Shao Yanjun, *Qinxie de wenxue chang* (The unbalanced literary field), (Nanjing: Jiangsu renming chubanshe, 2003), 258–299.

37 "Mian Mian: jiuge mubiao de yuwang" (Mian Mian: nine objects of desire), 26 October 2003, http://she.563.cn/article/2003/2003-10-26/606.html (accessed December 12, 2004).

38 "Shei jiao wo meinü zuojia wojiu gen shei guobuqu" (I am not happy at those who call me a beauty writer), http://www.booker.com. cn /gb/paper54/1/class005400034/hwz103335.htm (accessed December 12, 2004).

39 Angela McRobbie, "Shut up and Dance: Youth Culture and Changing Modes of Femininity," *Cultural Studies* 7, no. 3 (1993): 406–426.

40 Mian Mian, *Candy*, 184.

41 "Mian Mian: jiejin wuxian touming de hongse" (Mian Mian: getting close to the endlessly transparent red), http://www.dragonsource.com/tuijian/ mianmian.htm (accessed November 14, 2004).

42 Ibid.

43 Mian Mian, *"Feichang fumu"* (Extraordinary parents), in *Shejiao wu* (Social dance) (Bejing: Xin shijie chubanshe, 2002): 18–19.

44 "Mian Mian yi paidui de mingyi shenghuo" (Mian Mian lives in the name of party), *Jingping gouwu zhinan*, 11 July 2004, http://www.92china.com/ Htmls/Consumed/nblife/20040711210133.htm (accessed November 11, 2004).

45 Mian Mian, *Shejiao wu* (Social dance) (Bejing: Xin shijie chubanshe, 2002).

46 Mian Mian, *"Xiari li zuihou de meigui"* (The last rose of summer), in *Shejiao wu*, 294–297.

47 "Mian Mian jiedong zhihou tuichu shejiao wu" (Mian Mian wrote *Social Dance* after the ban is lifted), 16 May 2002, http://cul.sina.com.cn/s/2002-05-16/12826.html (accessed November 11, 2004).

48 Chun Shu is the author of *Beijing wawa* (Beijing doll). Her aspiration to prestigious institutes can be seen in Wang Jing and Shao Yanjun's discussions. See Wang Jing, "Youth Culture, Music, and Cell phone Branding in China," *Global Media and Communication* 1, no. 2 (2005): 185–201. Also see Shao Yanjun, "'Meinüwenxue' xianxiang yanjiu' (Study on "beauty literature" phenomenon), (Guilin: Guangxi shifan daxue chubanshe, 2005).

Chapter Three
Cyber Writing as Urban Fashion

1 Fletcher, Gordon. "Better than (Real)Life: Cyberspace as Urban Space," September 1997, http://www.spaceless.com/papers/10.htm (accessed December 12, 2004).

2 There was little follow-up information on the "four beauty writers" as well as the ambitious plan of "Bookoo." The four writers, like other beauty writers, seemed to disappear from the public view quickly.

3 Meng Jinwei, "Shangye baozhuang cuisheng 'meinü zuojia.'"

4 Barrie Sherman and Phil Judkins, *Glimpses of Heaven, Visions of Hell: Visual Reality and Its Implications* (London: Hodder and Stoughton, 1992).

5 Elwes, C. "Gender and Technology," *Variant* 15, 1993. Quoted in *Cyberspace/Cyberbodies/Cyberpunk*, ed. Mike Featherstone and Roger Burrows (London: Sage. 1995), 12–13.

6 Kevin Robin, "Cyberspace and the World We Live in," in *Cyberspace/Cyberbodies/Cyberpunk*, ed. Mike Featherstone and Roger Burrows, 136–155. Faith Wilding, "Where is the Feminism in Cyberfeminism?" 1998, http://www.obn.org.cfundef/faith_def.html (accessed November 12,2004).

7 The term "utopian, dystopian and heterotopian possibilities" is from *Cyberspace/Cyberbodies/Cyberpunk*. See Featherstone and Burrows, ed. *Cyberspace/Cyberbodies/Cyberpunk*, 1.

8 The statistics, data and survey are available at the website of China Internet Network Information Center. http://www.cnnic.net.cn/index/0E/00/ 11/index.htm. I especially retrieved the statistics from http://www.cnnic.net.cn/ download/2003/10/13/91748.pdf, and did the mathematic calculation myself. I retrieved the information on 24 December 2004.

9 *Selected Works of Mao Tse-Tung*, vol. 1 (Beijing: Foreign Language Press, 1964), 15.

[10] See Du Zuobing, "Nüxing sanwen de zhuanzhe dian" (Turning point of women's essays), 1 July 2002, http://www.china-woman.com/gb/2002/07/01/zgfnb/dssd/2.htm (accessed December 24, 2004).

[11] Cited from the book introduction on *Gediao*, http://dadao.net /htm/book/newbook/htm/0531/005.htm (accessed December 24, 2004).

[12] "Jiang Zemin's Speech at the Meeting Celebrating the 80th Anniversary of the Founding of the Communist Party of China," 1 July 2001, http://www.china.org.cn/e–speech/a.htm (accessed 26 December 2004).

[13] Ge Hongbing, "Neilian de yuwang." (Restrained desire), In *Fense de biaoqing* (Pink expression), ed. Ge Hongbing (Beijing: Beijing wenhua yishu chubanshe, 2002), 1–3.

[14] Bao Xiaoguang, *Xiaozi qingdiao* (Petit bourgeoisie taste) (Changchun: Jilin sheying chubanshe, 2002).

[15] Li Zhengliang, "Taipei, Shanghai he zhongguo xiaozi" (Taipei, Shanghai and Chinese petit bourgeoisie), http://www.srcs.nctu.edu.tw/CSA2005/papers/0108_A1_1_Li.pdf (accessed December 27, 2004).

[16] The survey was led by Zhou Xiaohong. His team categorized "middle class" by the standards of profession, education and incomes. See Zhou Xiaohong, ed. *Zhongguo zhongchan jieceng diaocha*, (Beijing: Shehui Kexue wenxian chubanshe, 2005). I am using the electronic version of the book, http://book.sina.com.cn/nzt/fin/zhongguozhongchanjieceng/3.shtml (accessed February 2, 2006).

[17] Huang Haibo, *Xiaozi nüren* (Petit bourgeois women) (Beijing: huawen chubanshe, 2002). Lao Le, ed. *Qin'ai xiaozi: guanyu yige bu queding qunluo de N zhong bu queding miaoshu* (Dear petit bourgeoisie: n types of ambiguous portrayal of an ambiguous group) (Beijing: xin shijie chubanshe, 2003). Xiao Xue, ed. *Xiaozi fengqing: kangnaixin xiandai nüxing shenghuo xiaobaike* (Petit bourgeois's taste: carnation modern women's life encyclopedia) (Nanjing: Nanjing chubanshe, 2003). Peng Jianze, ed. *Meiti jianfei shipu/xiaozi shenghuo shipu* (Recipes of beautifying bodies and losing weight /petit bourgeois's Recipes) (Changsha, Hunan renming chubanshe.1998).

[18] Mian Mian's personal webpage is www.mianmian.com, and Wei Hui's is http://goldnets.myrice.com/wh.

[19] Homepage, www.rongshu.com (accessed November 11, 2004).

[20] "Wenxue wangzhan fazhan: wangluo wenxue zouxiang guimohua fazhan," (The development of literature website: Internet literature becomes formal.) http://www.chinahtml.com/management/4/2006/gren-11428150143956.shtml (accessed April 20, 2006). Also see Ge Hongbin, ed. *Yige nüren de qige cemian: xinshiji wangluo xiaoshuo jingxuan* (Seven profiles of a woman: selected works of the new-age cyber fiction). Beijing: Zhongguo wenlian chebanshe, 2003.

[21] Li Gan, Xiong Jialiang and Cai Shuxian, ed. *Zhongguo dangdai wenxueshi* (History of contemporary Chinese literature) (Beijing: Kexue chubanshe, 2004).

[22] Ge Hongbing, "Zhimian wenxue de kuibai he wangluo wenxue de xingqi" (The collapse of literature on paper and the rise of the writings on the Internet), in *Zhengwu de shixue* (Shanghai, Shiji chuban jituan, 2001), 239–251.

[23] Chen Pingyuan, *Dangdai Zhongguo renwen guancha* (The observation of the contemporary Chinese humanity) (Beijing, Renming wenxue chubanshe, 2004), 106.

[24] Yi Wen, "Wangluo jiushi richang shenghuo: Zhou Jieru tan wangluo" (Internet is daily life: Zhou Jieru talks about the Internet). http://culture.netbig.com/topic/ 935/20000605/29011.htm (accessed December 29, 2004). Zhou Jieru, born in 1976, was a member of the Changzhou writers' association.

[25] Zhou Jieru, *Xiao Yao de Wang* (Xiao Yao's net) (Shenyang: Chunfeng wenyi chubanshe, 2000), 1.

[26] Ibid., 241.

[27] Ibid., 303.

[28] Ibid., 201.

[29] Marjorie Worthington, "Bodies That Natter: Virtual Translations and Transmissions of the Physical." *Critique: Studies in Contemporary Fiction*, 43:2 (2002 Winter), 192–208.

[30] Zhao Jinhua, "Zuojia shangwang ganshenme" (What writers do on the Internet), http://www.linlins.com/NewMoon/2/2000-07-21-23-45-11.html (accessed December 14, 2004).

[31] Zhou Jieru, *Xiao Yao de Wang*, 257–258.

[32] Yiwen, "Wangluo jiushi richang shenghuo: Zhou Jieru tan wangluo," http://culture.netbig.com/topic/935/20000605/29011.htm (accessed December 29, 2004).

[33] "Anni Baobei fangtan: leng yu ren, lian yu wu" (Anni Baobei interview: feeling cold towards people and passionate about materials), *Beijing qingnian zhoukan* (Beijing youth weekly), 11 November 2004, http://cul.sina.com.cn/s/2004-11-11/92653.html (accessed December 27, 2004).

[34] Ah Mei, "xiaozi wuyu: bushi jiao ni zuo xiaozi" (Petit bourgeoisie story: not a guide to becoming petit bourgeoisie), 8 October 2004, http://www.qdgdb.com/BaiWei/20041008/105642.htm (accessed December 28, 2004).

[35] Zheng Guoqing, "Anni Baobei, 'xiaozi' wenhua yu wenxue changyu de bianhua," (Anni Baobei, xiaozi culture and the changing Literary field), *Dangdai zuojia pinlun* 6 (2003): 74–79.

[36] Anni Baobei, *Gaobie wei'an* (Goodbye, Vivian) (Haikou: Nanhai chuban gongsi, 2002).

[37] Mao Jian, "Xiaozi shi zenyang liancheng de" (How *xiaozi* is tempered), http://www.cul-studies.com/asp/list2.asp?id=1375&writer=maojian (accessed December 30, 2004).

[38] Cadora, Karen. "Feminist Cyberpunk." *Science Fiction Studies* 22 (1995): 357–372.

Chapter Four
Glamorously Intellectual: An Intertextual Reading of Wei Hui

[1] "Wei Hui fangtan," (An interview with Wei Hui), http:// www.54youth .com.cn/ gb/ paper107/zt/xyzt/WH04.htm (accessed February 20, 2005).

2 Aijun Zhu and Sheldon Lu have written on Wei Hui and the "beauty writer" phenomenon. Zhu focuses on the inter-connectedness of authors, the mass media, and literary and cultural critics. She points out the "dead end of state-sanctioned nationalistic feminism" and calls for a feminist critique of sexuality. Lu places beauty writers in the context of "global biopolitics," and examines collective desire at a personal level. My focus in this chapter is to critique Wei Hui's cultural position against the backdrop of the increasingly blurred boundary between the elite and the popular. For details of Zhu and Lu's essays, see, Aijun Zhu, *Feminism and Global Chineseness: the Cultural Production of Controversial Women Authors* (Youngstown, NY.: Cambria Press, 2007): 109–174. Sheldon Lu, *Chinese Modernity and Global Biopolitics: Studies in Literature and Visual Culture* (Honolulu: University of Hawai'i Press: 2007): 53–70.

3 *Yuwang hua xiezuo*, literallytranslates as "*desirized* writing." It means the writings focus on all sorts of desires: material wealth, fame, sexual pleasure, and more.

4 Wei Hui, "Wo hai xiang zenme ne," 25.

5 Chen Pingyuan, *Dangdai Zhongguo renwen guancha* (Observation of Contemporary Chinese humanities) (Beijing: Renming wenxue chubanshe, 2004), 1.

6 For a detailed account of the high culture fever of the 1980s, see Jing Wang, *High Culture Fever* (Berkeley: University of California Press, 1996).

7 Yan Jiayan in 1995 offered a course "Study of Jin Yong's novels" in Beijing University.

8 Cui Jian's "Yiwu suoyou" (Nothing to my name) and "Zher de kongjian" (Space here) are included in *Bainian Zhongguo wenxue jingdian: 1979–1989*, vol. 7 edited by Xie Mian and Qian Liqun. See pages 47–49.

9 In *Zhongguo xiandai wenxue sanshi nian* (Thirty years of Chinese modern literature), the college literature textbook written by Qian Liqun, Wen Rumin and Wu Fuhui, included "*su,*" or "popular," novels from 1917 to 1949. See Qian Liqun, Wen Rumin and Wu Fuhui, *Zhongguo xiandai wenxue sanshi nian* (Beijing: Bejing daxue chubanshe, 1998).

10 See the title page of *Zuojia zazhi* (October 2000). Quote in Shao Yanjun, *Qinxie de wenxue chang*, 49.

11 Zhang Dachun, "Yao shui haokan" (Who is pleasant to read?), *Beijing wenxue*, no 1 (1999), Quoted in Shao Yanjun, *Qingxie de wenxuechang*, 81.

12 Xing Xiaofang, "Yipi nianqing nü zuojia zhanlu toujiao" (A group of young female writers stand out), *Writer* (July 1998), back inside cover.

13 Wei Hui. *Shanghai baby*, Trans. Bruce Humes (New York: Pocket Books, 2001),19.

14 Ibid., 1.

15 Wei Hui, "Crazy Like Wei Hui," in *Shuizhong de chunü* (A virgin in the water) (Shijiazhuang: huashan wenyi chubanshe, 2000), 177.

16 The "super market" exhibition, held on the fourth floor of a super market on April 10, 1999, was organized by two Chinese artists and a German artist. See Chen Xiaoyun, "Xiaofei "( )" de canyu: 'chaoshi' yishu zhanhua" (Consume the residual of "( ):" 'Super Market' art exhibition), http://www.wenxue.com/scene/arts/018.htm (accessed July 14, 2005).

17 Deirdre Sabina Knight, "Shanghai Cosmopolitan: Class, Gender, and Cultural Citizenship in Weihui's *Shanghai Babe*," *Journal of Contemporary China* 12, no. 37 (November 2003), 640.

18 Wei Hui, *Shanghai Baby*, 70.

19 "Wei Hui de zitai and Mian Mian de shengming" (Wei Hui's attitude and Mian Mian's announcement,) 14 Aprile 2000, http://www.white-collar.net/wx_wxf/wxf04/161.htm (accessed January 8, 2005).

20 Wei Hui, *Shanghai Baby*, the dedication page.

21 Wei Hui, "Bushi wo tai linglei, shi tamen tai zhuliu," (It is not that I am unconventional. It is the fact that they are too mainstream), *Zhongguo qingnian bao*, 20 March 2000 3. Cited in Xiao Jianhua, "Guanyu Wei Hui he Mian Mian deng 'qishi niandai hou' zuojia de sikao," (Thoughts on 'post seventies' writers such as Wei Hui and Mian Mian), 9 November 2004, http://www.culstudies.com/ rendanews/displaynews.asp?id=4040 (accessed January 15, 2005).

22 Wei Hui, *Shanghai Baby*, 24–25.

23 Zhang Ailing, *Yuannü*, 434. Cited from Zhang Yingjin, *The City in Modern Chinese Literature and Film* (Stanford, CA.: Stanford University Press, 1996), 242

24 Janet Ng, *The Experience of Modernity: Chinese Autobiography of the Early Twentieth Century* (Ann Arbor: University of Michigan Press, 2003), 66–67.

25 Deirdre Sabina Knight, "Shanghai Cosmopolitan: Class, Gender, and Cultural Citizenship in Weihui's *Shanghai Babe*," 640.

26 "Neirong gediao dixia de 'meinü wenxue' bei jing." ("Beauty literature" with low–grade content and taste was banned), 15 June 2000, http://edu.sina.com.cn/wander/2000-06-15/4584.shtml (accessed February 20, 2005).

27 Wei Hui, "Crazy Like Wei Hui," 229–230.

28 "Li Dawei vs. Wei Hui: Gei suo juzhu de chengshi tushang yiceng fenhong se," (Li Dawei vs. Wei Hui: apply some pink color to the city in which we live), 15 September 2004, http://edu.sina.com.cn/wander/2000-09-15/12271.shtml (accessed January 10, 2005).

29 By examining urban-oriented modernist writings and leftist texts in Shanghai of the 1930s, Zhang Yingjin discovered that the female is generally absent in the male-authored texts. Male writers and film makers always made female protagonists disappear. However, women writers such as Zhang Ailing and Su Qin were also active in establishing female subjectivities. See Zhang, *The City in Modern Chinese Literature and Film* (Stanford, CA.: Stanford University Press, 1996), 155–231.

30 Wei Hui, *Shanghai Baby*, 25.

31 Ibid., 14.

32 Ibid., 1.

33 "Wei Hui fang tan" (An interview with Wei Hui), http://www.54youth.com.cn/gb/paper107/zt/xyzt/WH04.htm (accessed February 20, 2005).

34 Wei Hui seems to echo the late Qing dynasty ti/yong (substance/function) opposition, articulated by Zhang Zhidong, where Chinese learning is regarded as the cultural core and Western learning as the instrumental. Yet the late Qing national enlightenment discourse is revised at the personal level by Wei Hui. Her approach to cultural difference is more pragmatic and utilitarian.

35 Wei Hui, *Shanghai Baby*, 173.

36 Ibid., 24.

37 Ibid., 23.

38 Ibid., 2.

39 Wei Hui, "Wo haixiang zenme ne?" 25.

40 Wei Hui, *Shanghai Baby*, 177.

41 Ibid., 104.

42 Ibid., 177.

43 "Wei Hui he Zhang Yuan de duihua: xiangle zhuyi zhe de 'linghun show'" (The dialogue between Wei Hui and Zhang Yuan: 'the soul show' of the hedonists), 29 September 2004, http://culture.china.com/zh_cn/reading/writer/11022791 /2004092 9/11898679_1.html (accessed January 15, 2005).

44 See the cover page of *Shanghai Baby*, trans. Bruce Humes (New York: Pocket Books, 2001).

45 See the cover image, *Shanghai Baobei* (Shenyang: Chunfeng wenyi chubanshe, 1999).

46 See cover image of *Shanghai Baby* (New York: Pocket Books, 2001).

47 *Feidu* (Faded Capital), written by Jia Pingwa, is on a man's sexual relation with several women in his life.

48 "Wei Hui he *Shanghai Baobei*" (Wei Hui and *Shanghai Baby*), http:// edu.sina.com.cn/2000-05-05/5/33.html (accessed April 4, 2005).

49 Jason Cowley, "Bridget Jones with Blow Jobs: Interview with Chinese Novelist Zhou Wei Hui," *New Statesman*, 23 July 2001, 52.

50 Richard Brooks, "China's Little Red Book of Sex and the City," *The Sunday Times*, 3 June 2001, 4.

51 See the reviews on the back cover of *Shanghai Baby*.

52 Wei Hui, *Shanghai Baobei*, http://www.bookfree.com.cn/aiqing/wh-shang/ 33.htm (accessed April 5, 2005).

53 The Chinese title of *Marrying Buddha* is "Wo de chan" (My zen). See Wei Hui, *Wo de chan*, (Shanghai: Shanghai wenyi chubanshe, 2004).

54 "Compromising Position for One Shanghai Writer: Wei Hui Mixes Steamy Sex with a Love of China," *Asia Africa Intelligence Wire*, 24 October 2004.

Chapter Five
Body Writing

1 Ge Hongbing claimed he did not know Cixous's body writing theory when he studied the writings of new humanity writers. He said he was concerned with the contemporary literary phenomenon in China, and he was also influenced by a Chinese friend who had studied the "philosophy of the body." See Gui Jie, "Wo xiwang zhege shehui geng kuanrong: yu Ge Hongbing tan *Sha Chuang*" (I hope the society is more lenient: a talk with Ge Hongbing on *Bed of Sand*), *Qingnian cankao* (Youth reference), 17 February 2004, http://news.sina.com.cn/s/2004-02-17/12352884198.shtml (accessed May 8, 2006).

2 Hélène Cixous, "The Laugh of the Medusa," *Signs* 1, no. 4 (Summer 1976), 875–893.

3 Helene Cixous, 876.

4 Ibid.

5 Ibid., 880.

6   Ibid., 877.

7   Ibid., 885.

8   Ge Hongbing, "Geti wenhua shidai yu shenti xing zuojia" (The era of individual culture and body writers), 22 October 2003, http://www.culstudies.com/ rendanews/displaynews.asp?id=1746 (accessed October 20, 2005).

9   Ibid.

10 Ge Hongbing, "Guanyu shachuang de yidian zhibaihua" (Some frank words on bed of sand), 11 December 2003, http://www.xiaoyan.com/ c/c_title_disp.cfm?tn=132&un=106 (accessed October 20, 2005).

11 Ge Hongbing said this when he was interviewed by Phoenix TV anchorwoman Xu Gehui. See "Ge Hongbing," 1 September 2004, http://www. phoenixtv.com/phoenixtv/76563401278488576/20040901/296688.shtml (accessed October 22, 2005).

12 Xie Youshun. Shenti Xiuci (Body rhetoric) (Guangzhou: Huacheng chubanshe, 2003).

13 Meng Zi, "Mencius," in The Chinese Classics, Vol. 1 & II, trans. James Legge (Taibei Shi: Nantian shu ju): 411.

14 Xie Youshun, Shenti xiuci, 28.

15 Yu Hua, "One King of Reality." Tr. Jeanne Tai. In David Der-wei Wang, ed., Running Wild: New Chinese Writers (New York: Columbia University Press, 1994), 65.

16 Ibid., 30–34. Poet Xi Chuan suggested that "xia ban shen" (lower part of the body) is just a sensational term to catch the attention of the media. What the poets have been doing is actually serious intellectual engagement, besides the exploration of the corporality. For example, some of the poets went to the rural area and investigated the problems of AIDS. Xi Chuan gave the talk on August 7, 2005, at a Conference "Comparative Modernisms: Empire, Aesthetics and History" held by Tsinghua University and University of Michigan.

17 Shen Haobo, "Xia ban shen xiezuo ji fandui shang ban shen" (Write the lower part of the body and oppose the upper part of the body), in 2000 Zhongguo xinshi nianjian (Year book of Chinese new poetry in 2000), ed. Yang Ke (Guangzhou: Guangzhou chubanshe, 2001), 544–547.

18 Yin Lichuan, "Weishenme bu zai shufu yidian" (Why not be more comfortable), 31 January 2000, http://www.wenxue2000.com/poet/ylc.htm (accessed September 20, 2005). The Chinese term "shufu," which I translate as "comfortable" for the sake of the grammar and poetic rhythm, has a wide range of implications that includes the "sexually pleasurable." Most of the poems of "writing lower part of the body" can be found on a website Shi jiang hu (The river and lake of poems) at http://www.wenxue2000.com/.

19 Xie Youshun, Shenti xiuci, 40–42.

20 Xie Youshun: Shenti xiuci, 28.

21 Ge Hongbing, "Shenti xiezuo – Qimeng xushi, geming xushi zhihou: 'shenti' de dangxia chujing" (Body writing: after narratives of enlightenment and revolution: the contemporary condition of the "body,") Dangdai wentan (Contemporary literary forum) (March 2005):3–9.

22 See Ge Hongbing's online interview, 5 June 2002, http://www.people.com.cn/GB/14738/14761/25876/1719155.html (accessed October 2, 2005).

23 Ta Ai, *Shi da meinu zuojia pipan shu* (Criticizing ten beauty writers) (Beijing: Hualing chubanshe, 2005), 1–2.

24 Ibid., 4.

25 Ibid., 5.

26 "Shenti xiezuo yu xingwei yishu: Muzi Mei, Jiu Dan, Wei Hui, Mian Mian, Chunshu" (Body writing and performing arts: Muzi Mei, Jiu Dan, Wei Hui and Mian Mian), 12 August 2004, http://www.culstudies.com/ rendanews/ displaynews.asp? id=3414 (accessed October 20, 2005).

27 Jiu Dan, "Yiben guanyu zui'e de shu: yu youren de duihua" (A book on sin: converse with a friend), in *Wu Ya* (Crow) (Wuhan: Changjiang wenyi chubanshe, 2000), 6.

28 "Mian Mian zibai: xiezuo de 'shenti xing' bushi yuwang" (Mian Mian's confession: body writing is not the desire), http://www.booker.com.cn /gb/paper54/1/class005400034/hwz103339.htm (accessed October 22, 2005).

29 Hélène Cixous, "The Laugh of the Medusa," 877.

30 Meng Jinwei, "Shangye baozhuang cuisheng 'meinü zuojia.'"

31 "Zhiming pinglunjia zuojia shou Wei Hui," (Famous critics and writers comment on Wei Hui), 23 April 2000, http://edu.sina.com.cn/critique/2000-04-23/2192.shtml (accessed February 6, 2005).

32 Liu Jianmei. *Revolution Plus Love* (Honolulu: University of Hawai'i Press, 2003), 24.

33 Ibid

34 Ibid.

35 For detailed discussion on the politics of gender identity, see Tze-lan D. Sang, *The Emerging Lesbian: Famle Same–Sex Desire* in *Modern China* (Chicago: University of Chicago Press, 2003).

36 My personal interview with Li Jingze on July 29, 2004.

37 Wei Wei, "Yige nianling de xing yishi" (Sexual consciousness at different ages), *Xiaoshuo jie* (Fiction world) 5, (1997), 165–168.

38 Ibid, 166.

39 Zhao Bo, "Guanyu xing, yu Shasha tanxin" (About sex, confide with Shasha), *Xiaoshuo jie* (Fiction world), no. 6 (1997).

40 Muzi Mei originally published her sex diary dated between June and November 2003 on a "blogcn" website. Since then, several versions of her blog have appeared on different websites. The original one is already hard to locate on the web. The diary I am quoting is from several websites and discussion forums, in the hope of getting a relatively complete version.

41 Muzi Mei, "Lunli pian" (Ethical film), 4 July 2003, http://www.zzhot.com/text/ xing030704.htm (accessed October 25, 2005).

42 Muzi Mei, "Zou nar shui nar" (Sleep wherever you go), http://bbs.cer.net/ archive/ index.php/t–126604.html (accessed October 25, 2005).

43 Muzi Mei, "Hanlao baoshou" (Ensure the harvest), 27 June 2003, http:// www.zzhot.com/text/xing030627.htm (accessed October 25, 2005).

44 Muzi Mei, *Diary*, 7 November 2003, http://www.xishui.net/tonepop/ com/muzimei /muzimei0.htm (accessed October 20, 2005)

[45] Muzi Mei, *Diary*, 6 November 2003, http://www.xishui.net/tonepop/ com/muzimei /muzimei0.htm (accessed October 20, 2005)

[46] "Muzi Mei zhuanti" (Special column on Muzi Mei), http://www.zzhot.com/text/ xing.htm (accessed October 25, 2005).

[47] Muzi Mei, *Diary*, 3 November 2003, http://www.xishui.net/ tonepop/com/ muzimei /muzimei0.htm (accessed October 20, 2005)

[48] "Jiedu Muzi Mei, (Reading Muzi Mei), *Dadi* (Earth), no. 23 (2004), http://www. people.com.cn/GB/paper81/11029/999184.html (accessed October 27, 2005).

[49] "Zhuying qingtong" was a college teacher. She posted in her blog her naked pictures and journals reflecting body, sex and emotion. She said she just returned the body to its basic form as an "object" (*wuti*). See the blog of "Zhuying Qingtong" at http://castle3.tianyablog.com. "Sister Lotus" posted various pictures of herself dancing or flirting first on the discussion forums of Beijing University and Tsinghua University. Her perfect confidence over her not-so-perfect body initially drew laughs and curses, and eventually turned her into an Internet legend.

[50] According to a report on CNN, many formerly "small" and traditionally chic topics have found a public space on weblogs, and therefore enable more women to speak up about their daily lives. See "Pundits and knitters find common ground in Web logs," http://www.cnn.com/2005/TECH/Internet/08/ 10/mena.trott/ (accessed December 23, 2005).

[51] Chen Jia, "Cong 'Muzi Mei' xianxiang kan bokewang dui nüxing huayu kongjian de tuozhan" (The extension of women's discoursive space in the case of "Muzi Mei"), 18 June 2004, http://www.woxie.com/article/list.asp?id=16673 (accessed October 18, 2005).

[52] "Ge Hongbing tan *shachuang*" (Ge Hongbing talks about *Bed of Sand*), 15 December 2003, http://book.sina.com.cn/1071464102_shachuang/2003-12-15/3/ 30925.shtml (accessed September 3, 2005).

Conclusion

[1] Wang Shuo, "Wang Shuo Chen Ran duiha lu" (Dialogue between Wang Shuo and Chen Ran," 28 March 2002, http://www.culture.zju.edu.cn/ new/html/1/10/20/20020328/004702_3.html (accessed August 3, 2003).

[2] Chen Li, "Zhu Dake: Zhe shi yige wenxue jiaochun de shidai" (Zhu Dake: this is an ear when literature moans), *Beijing qingnian zhoukan* (Beijing youth weekly), 25 November 2003, http://www.people.com.cn/ GB/14738/14754/ 4765/ 2213181.html (accessed November 5, 2005).

[3] The publisher, Changjiang wenyi chubanshe, printed 50,000 copies of the book, which was a large number for novels. See Hu Liuming, "Zhongguo jingru qingse jingji shidai le ma" (Does China enter the stage of pornography economy), http://news.xinhuanet.com/book/2003-11/07/content_1165512.htm (accessed November 5, 2005).

[4] Ge Hongbing, "Ge Hongbing shengming" (Ge Hongbing's announcement), 11 December 2003, http://www.culstudies.com/ rendanews/ displaynews.asp? id= 2006 (accessed November 1, 2005).

[5] Meng Jinwei, "Shangye baozhuang cuisheng 'meinü zuojia.'"

6   Shi Zhanjun, "Gaobie xinsheng dai" (Farewell, new generation), *Xiaoshuo pinglun* (Fiction critique) 3, (2001): 92–93. The "new generation" in Shi's essay has a broader reference, referring to all the new literary voices, including "urban fiction" writers, "female private writing" and writers born in the seventies.

7   "Mian Mian reaches maturity with 'Panda Sex'," 1 March 2005, http://www.chinadaily.com.cn/english/doc/2005-03/01/content_420714.htm (accessed October 20, 2005).

8   Zhang Xinyin, "Yu shenghuo xiang huying: huiwang 2003 nian duanpian xiaoshuo" (In concert with life: retrospection on novellas of 2003), *Wenxue bao* (Literature newspaper), 5 January 2004, http://www.news365.com.cn/wxpd/ds/rdjj/t20040105_6250.htm (accessed October 29, 2005).

9   Shu Shu, "Di sanjie Lu Xun wenxue jiang gongbu, '70hou' zuojia shoujin zhuliu" (The third Lu Xun Literary Award publicized, and "post-seventies" writer mainstreamed for the first time," 29 December 2004, http://www.chinanews.com.cn/ news/2004/2004-12-29/26/522273.shtml (accessed October 27, 2005).

10   Shen Congwen, for example, depicted a child bride in "Xiao Xiao." See Shen Congwen, "Xiao Xiao," in *The Columbia Anthology of Modern Chinese Literature*, ed. Joseph S.M. Lau and Howard Goldblatt (New York: Columbia University Press, 1995), 97–111.

BIBLIOGRAPHY

Anni Baobei. *Bi'an hua* (Flowers at the distant shore). Haikou: Nanhai chuban gongsi, 2001.

——. *Gaobie wei'an* (Goodbye, Vivian). Haikou: Nanhai chuban gongsi, 2002.

"Anni Baobei fangtan: leng yu ren, lian yu wu" (Anni Baobei interview: feeling cold towards people and passionate about materials). *Beijing qingnian zhoukan* (Beijing youth weekly), 11 November 2004. http://cul.sina.com.cn/s/2004-11-11/92653.html (accessed December 27, 2004).

Alexander, Sally. *Becoming a Woman and Other Essays in 19th and 20th Century Feminist History*. London: Virago, 1994.

Annesley, James. *Blank Fictions: Consumerism, Culture, and the Contemporary American Novel*. New York: St. Martin's Press, 1998.

Appadurai, Arjun. *Modernity at Large: Cultural Dimensions of Globalization* Minneapolis: University of Minnesota Press, 1996.

Banet-weiser, Sarah. *The Most Beautiful Girl in the World: Beauty Pageants and National Identity*. Berkeley: University of California Press, 1999.

Barlow, Tani E, ed. *Gender Politics in Modern China: Writing and Feminism*. Durham, NC.: Duke University Press, 1993.

Bartky, Sandra Lee. "Narcissism, Femininity and Alienation." *Social Theory and Practice* 8, (Summer 1982): 137–138.

Bao Yaming, Wang Hongtu and Zhu Shengjian. *Shanghai jiuba: kongjian, xiaofei he xiangxiang* (Shanghai bars: space, consumption and imagination). Nanjing: Jiangsu renming chubanshe, 2001.

Bao Xiaoguang. *Xiaozi qingdiao* (Petit Bourgeoisie taste). Changchun: Jilin sheying chubanshe, 2002.

Beauvoir, Simone de. *The Second Sex*. Trans. H. M Parshley. New York: Alfred A. Knopf, 1953.

114

Bem, Sandra L. *The Lenses of Gender: Transforming the Debate on Sexual Inequality* New Haven, CT.: Yale University Press, 1993.

Berger, John. *Ways of Seeing.* New York: Viking Press, 1973.

Braidotti, Rosi. *Nomadic Subjects: Embodiment and Sexual Difference in Contemporary Feminist Theory.* New York: Columbia University Press, 1994.

Brand, Peg Zeglin, ed. *Beauty Matters.* Bloomington: Indiana University Press, 2000.

Brooks, Richard. "China's little red book of sex and the city." *The Sunday Times*, 3 June 2001, 4.

Brownell, Susan and Jeffrey N. Wasserstrom, ed. *Chinese Femininities, Chinese Masculinities: A Reader.* Berkeley: University of California Press, 2002.

Brumberg, Joan Jacobs. *The Body Project: An Intimate History of American Girls.* New York: Vintage Books, 1998.

Buckley, Cheryl and Hilary Fawcett. *Fashioning the Feminine: Representation and Women's Fashion from the Fin de Siècle to the Present.* London: I.B. Tauris, 2002.

Butler, Judith. *Gender Trouble: Feminism and the Subversion of Identity.* New York: Routledge, 1990.

Cadora, Karen. "Feminist Cyberpunk." *Science Fiction Studies* 22 (1995): 357–372.

Cagle, Van M. *Reconstructing Pop/Subculture: Art, Rock, and Andy Warhol.* Thousand Oaks, CA.: Sage Publications, 1995.

Cai Zhizhong. *Cai Zhizhong gudian manhua* (Cai Zhizhong's classical cartoon). Beijing: Shenghuo Dushu Xinzhi Sanlian shudian, 2001.

Can Xue, *Canglao de Fuyun* (Old cloud). Changchun: Shidai wenyi chubanshe, 2001.

"'Caoyang nianhua bei Taiwan meiti lieru Zhongguo shi da qingchun xiaoshuo" ("Life like grass" is listed as one of the ten youth novels by Taiwan media). 22 November 2003, http://book.sina.com.cn/news/c/2003-11-22/3/26128.shtml.

Chapkis, Wendy. *Beauty Secrets: Women and the Politics of Appearance.* Boston: South End Press, 1986.

Chen Dayan. *Shanghai de feng hua xue yue* (Shanghai's breeze, flower, snow and moon). Beijing: Zuojia chubanshe, 1998.

——. *Shanghai de hongyan yishi* (Shanghai beauty). Beijing: Zuojia chubanshe, 2000.

——. *Shanghai de jingzhi yuye* (Shanghai princess). Beijing: Zuojia chubanshe, 2001.

Chen Jia. "Cong 'Muzi Mei' xianxiang kan bokewang dui nüxing huayu kongjian de tuozhan" (The extension of the space of women's discourse in the case of "Muzi Mei"). 18 June 2004. http://www.woxie.com/article/list.asp?id=16673 (accessed October 18, 2005).

Chen Li. "Zhu Dake: Zhe shi yige wenxue jiaochun de shidai" (Zhu Dake: this is an era when literature moans). *Beijing qingnian zhoukan* (Beijing youth weekly), 25 November 2003. http://www.people.com.cn/GB/14738/14754/4765/2213181.html (accessed November 5, 2005).

Chen, Nancy N et al., ed. *China Urban: Ethnographies of Contemporary Culture*.Durham, NC.: Duke University Press, 2001.

——. "Zouxiang xin zhuangtai: dangdai dushi xiaoshuo de yanjin" (In a new status: the development of contemporary urban fiction). *Wenyi zhengming* (Literary discussion) 4 (1994): 22–34.

Chen, Peng-hsiang and Whitney Crothers Dilley, eds. *Feminism/Femininity in Chinese Literature*. New York: Rodopi, 2002.

Chen Pingyuan. *Dangdai Zhongguo renwen guancha* (The observation of the contemporary Chinese humanity). Beijing: Renming wenxue chubanshe, 2004.

Chen, Xiaomei. *Acting the Right Part: Political Theatre and Popular Drama in Contemporary China*. Honolulu: University of Hawai'I Press, 2002.

Chen Xiaoming. *Fangzhen de niandai: chaoxianshi wenxue liubian yu wenhua xiangxiang* (Virtue reality: the changing surreal literature and cultural imaginary). Taiyuan: Shangxi Jiaoyu chubanshe, 1999.

Cheng, Joseph Y.S., ed. *China in the Post-Deng Era*. Hong Kong: Chinese University Press, 1998.

Chow, Rey. *Primitive Passions*. New York: Columbia University Press, 1995.

Cixous, Hélène. "The Laugh of the Medusa." *Signs* 1, no. 4 (Summer, 1976): 875–893.

Conboy, Katie, Nadia Medina and Sarah Stanbury, eds. *Writing on the Body: Female Embodiment and Feminist Theory*. New York: Columbia University Press, 1997.

Cowley, Jason. "Bridget Jones with Blow Jobs: Interview with Chinese Novelist Zhou Weihui." *New Statesman*, 23 July 2001, 52.

Croll, Elisabeth. *Changing Identities of Chinese Women: Rhetoric, Experience, and Self-perception in Twentieth-Century China*. Hong Kong: Hong Kong University Press, 1995.

Cui Jian. "Yiwu suoyou" (Nothing to my name) and "Zher de kongjian" (Space here). In *Bainian Zhongguo wenxue jingdian*: (Classic Chinese Literature in one hundred years: 1979–1989), vol. 7, ed. Xie Mian and Qian Liqun. Beijing: Beijing daxue chubanshe. 1996. 47-49.

Dai Jinhua. *Yingxin shuxie* (Invisible writing). Nanjing: Jiangsu renming chubanshe, 1999.

——, ed. *Shuxie wenhua yingxiong* (Writing cultural heroes). Nanjing: Jiangsu renming chubanshe, 2000.

——. "Invisible Women: Contemporary Chinese Cinema and Women's Film." Trans., Mayfair Yang. *Position* 3, 1(spring 1995): 255–280.

Dai Lai. "Zhunbei hao le ma" (Are you ready). *Shouhuo* 3 (2000): 56–61.

Davis, Deborah S., ed. *The Consumer Revolution in Urban China*. Berkeley: University of California Press, 2000.

Dicker, Rory Cooke and Alison Piepmeier, eds. *Catching a Wave: Reclaiming Feminism for the 21st Century*. Boston: Northeastern University Press, 2003.

Dirlik, Arif and Xudong Zhang, ed. *Postmodernism & China*. Durham, NC.: Duke University Press, 2000.

Dolezelová-Velingerová, Milena. *The Chinese Novel at the Turn of the Century*. Toronto: University of Toronto Press, 1980.

Dutton, Michael, ed. *Streetlife China*. Cambridge, UK: Cambridge University Press, 1998.

Ebert, Teresa L. *Ludic Feminism and After: Postmodernism, Desire, and Labor in Late Capitalism*. Ann Arbor: University of Michigan Press, 1996.

Entwistle, Joanne. *The Fashioned Body: Fashion, Dress, and Modern Social Theory*. Malden: Polity Press. 2000.

Epstein, Jonathon S., ed. *Youth Culture: Identity in a Postmodern World*. Malden, MA.: Blackwell, 1998.

Farrer, James. *Opening Up: Youth Sex Culture and Market Reform in Shanghai*. Chicago: University of Chicago Press, 2002.

Fausto-Sterling, Anne. *Sexing the Body: Gender Politics and the Construction of Sexuality*. New York: Basic Books, 2000.

Featherstone, Mike and Roger Burrows, eds. *Cyberspace/Cyberbodies/Cyberpunk*. London: Sage, 1995.

Featherstone, Mike, Scott Lash and Roland Robertson, ed. *Global Modernities*. London: Sage, 1995.

Ferguson, Marjorie. *Forever Feminine: Women's Magazines and the Cult of Femininity*. London: Heinemann Educational Books LTD, 1983.

Ferry, Megan M. "Marketing Chinese Women Writers in the 1990s, or the Politics of Self-fashioning." *Journal of Contemporary China* 12, no. 37 (November 2003): 655–675.

Finnane, Antonia and Anne McLaren, eds. *Dress, Sex and Text in Chinese Culture*. Clayton, Australia: Monash Asia Institute, 1999.

Flanagan, Mary and Austin Booth eds. *Reload: Rethinking Women + Cyberculture*. Cambridge, MA: MIT Press, 2002.

Fletcher, Gordon. "'Better than (Real) Life': Cyberspace as Urban Space." September 1997, http://www.spaceless.com/papers/10.htm (accessed December 12, 2004).

Foucault, Michel. *The History of Sexuality, Volume I: An Introduction.* Trans. Robert Hurley. New York: Vintage Books, 1990.

——, *Language, Counter-Memory and Practice: Selected Essays and Interviews.* Trans. Donald F. Bouchard and Sherry Simon. Ithaca: Cornell University Press, 1980.

Fussell, Paul. *Class: A Guide Through the American Status System.* New York: Summit Books, 1983.

Gaines, Jane and Charlotte Herzog, ed. *Fabrications: Costume and the Female Body.* New York: Routledge, 1990.

Gammel, Irene, ed. *Confessional Politics: Women's Sexual Self-representations in Life Writing and Popular Media.* Carbondale: Southern Illinois University Press, 1999.

Gatens, Moira. *Imaginary Bodies: Ethics, Power and Corporeality.* New York: Routledge, 1996.

Ge Hongbing. *Zhengwu de shixue* (Poetics at noon). Shangha: Shiji chuban jituan, 2001.

——. *Shachuang* (Bed of sands). Wuhan: Changjiang wenyi chubanshe, 2003.

——. *Zhang'ai yu rentong* (Impediment and identification). Shanghai: Xuelin chubanshe: 2000.

——. "Neilian de yuwang" (Restrained desire). In *Fense de biaoqing: shi xiaozi nüzuojia jiexi* (Pink expression: analysis of ten female petit bourgeois writers), ed. Ge Hongbing. Beijing: Wenhua yishu chubanshe, 2002. 1-3

——. "Shenti xiezuo – Qimeng xushi, geming xushi zhihou: 'shenti' de dangxia chujing" (Body writing: after narratives of enlightenment and revolution: the contemporary condition of the "body"). *Dangdai wentan* (Contemporary literary forum) (March 2005):3–9.

——. "Mingmin de ganga – ye tan 'qishi niandai sheng zuojia.'" (Awkward naming: talk about born-in-the-seventies writers). *Nanfang wentan* (Southern literary forum), no. 6 (1998): 19–21.

——, ed. *Yige nüren de qige cemian: xinshiji wangluo xiaoshuo jingxuan* (Seven profiles of a woman: selected works of the new age cyber fiction). Beijing: wenlian chebanshe, 2003.

——. "Geti wenhua shidai yu shenti xing zuojia" (The era of individual culture and body writers). 22 October 2003. http://www.culstudies.com/rendanews/displaynews.asp?id=1746 (accessed October 20, 2005).

——. "Guanyu *shachuang* de yidian zhibaihua" (Some frank words on *bed of sand*). 11 December 2003. http://www.xiaoyan.com/c/c-title-disp.cfm? tn=132&un=106 (accessed October 20, 2005).

——. "Ge Hongbing shengming" (Ge Hongbing announcement). 11 December 2003. http://www.culstudies.com/rendanews/displaynews.asp?id=2006 (accessed November 1, 2005).

Genette, Gerard. "Introduction to the Paratext." *New Literary History* 22, no. 2 (Spring 1991): 261–272.

——. *Paratexts: Thresholds of Interpretation.* Cambridge: Cambridge University Press, 1997.

Gilmartin, Christina K., Gail Hershatter, Lisa Rofel, and Tyrene White, eds. *Engendering China: Women, Culture, and the State.* Cambridge: Harvard University Press, 1994.

Greene, Gayle. *Changing the Story: Feminist Fiction and the Tradition.* Bloomington: Indiana University Press, 1991.

Grosz, Elizabeth. *Volatile Bodies: Toward a Corporeal Feminism.* Bloomington: Indiana University Press, 1994.

"Guanzhu Muzi mei" (Focus on Muzi Mei). http://news.sina.com.cn/z/ mzmrfb/index.shtml (accessed October 20, 2005).

Gui Jie. "Wo xiwang zhege shehui geng kuanrong: yu Ge Hongbing tan *Sha Chuang*" (I hope the society is more lenient: a talk with Ge Hongbing on *Bed of Sand*). *Qingnian cankao* (Youth reference), 17 February 2004. http://news.sina.com.cn/s /2004-02-17/ 12352884198.shtml (accessed May 8, 2006).

Hall, Christine. *Daughters of the Dragon: Women's Lives in Contemporary China.* London: Scarlet Press, 1997.

Han Ziyong. "Dushi mengjing he zhongchan jieji xiezuo" (Cosmopolitan dream and the middle-class writing). *Dangdai zuojia pinglun* (Criticism on contemporary writers) no. 3 (1996): 121–123.

Heywood, Leslie and Jennifer Drake, eds. *Third Wave Agenda: Being Feminist, Doing Feminism.* Minneapolis: University of Minnesota Press, 1997.

Honig, Emily and Gail Hershatter. *Personal Voices: Chinese Women in the 1980's.* Stanford, CA.: Stanford University Press, 1988.

Hu Liuming. "Zhongguo jingru qingse jingji shidai le ma" (Does China enter the stage of pornographic economy). http://news. xinhuanet. com/ book/2003-11/ 07/ content-1165512.htm (accessed November 5, 2005).

Hu, Ying. "Writing Erratic Desire: Sexual Politics in Contemporary Chinese Fiction." *In Pursuit of Contemporary East Asian Culture*, ed. Xiaobing Tang and Stephen Snyder. Boulder, CO.: Westview Press, 1996. 49–68.

——, *Tales of Translation: Composing the New Woman in China, 1899–1918*. Stanford, CA.: Stanford University Press, 2000.

Huang Haibo. *Xiaozi nüren* (Petit bourgeois women). Beijing: Huawen chubanshe, 2002.

Huang Shuqin. "A Conversation with Huang Shuqin." *Position* 3 (Winter 1995), 790–805.

Jameson, Fredric. "Notes on Globalization as a Philosophical Issue." In *The Culture of Globalization*, ed. Fredric Jameson and Masao Miyoshi. Durham, NC.: Duke University Press, 1998. 54–77.

——. "The Cultural Logic of Late Capitalism." In *From Modernism to Postmodernism: An Anthology*, ed. Lawrence E. Cahoone. Cambridge, MA.: Blackwell Publishers, 1996. 564–574.

Jiang, Hong. "The Masculine–Feminine Woman: Transcending Gender Identity in Zhang Xinxin's Fiction." *China Information* 15, 1 (2001): 138–165.

"Jiang Zemin's Speech at the Meeting Celebrating the 80th Anniversary of the Founding of the Communist Party of China." 1 July 2001. http://www.china.org.cn/e-speech/a.htm.

Jiu Da. *Wu Ya* (Crow). Wuhan: Changjiang wenyi chubanshe, 2000.

King, Debra Walker. *Body politics and the Fictional Double*. Bloomington: Indiana University Press, 2000.

Kloet, Jeroen de. "'Let Him Fucking See the Green Smoke beneath My Groin': The Mythology of Chinese Rock. In *Postmodernism and China*, ed. Dirlik, Arif and Zhang Xudong. Durham, NC.: Duke University Press, 2000. 239–274.

Knight, Deirdre Sabina. "Shanghai Cosmopolitan: Class, Gender, and Cultural Citizenship in Weihui's *Shanghai Babe*." *Journal of Contemporary China* 12, no. 37 (November 2003): 639–653.

Lambert, Ellen Zetzel. *The Face of Love, Feminism and the Beauty Question*. Boston: Beacon Press, 1995.

Lang, Miriam. "San Mao and Qiong Yao, a 'Popular' Pair." *Modern Chinese Literature and Culture* 15, no. 2: 76–120.

Lao Le, ed. *Qin'ai xiaozi: guanyu yige bu queding qunluo de N zhong bu queding miaoshu* (Dear petit bourgeoisie: n types of ambiguous portrayal of an ambiguous group). Beijing: Xin shijie chubanshe, 2003.

Laozhao pian (Old pictures). Jinan: Shandong huabao chubanshe. 1997–2006.

Larson, Wendy. *Women and Writing in Modern China*. Stanford, CA.: Stanford University Press, 1998.

Lau, Jenny Kwok Wah. "Globalization and Youthful Subculture: The Chinese Sixth-Generation Films at the Dawn of the New Century." In *Multiple Modernity: Cinemas and Popular Media in Transcultural East*

Asia, ed. Lau, Jenny Kwok Wah. Philadelphia: Temple University Press, 2003. 13–27.

Leidholdt, Dorchen. *The Sexual Liberals and the Attack on Feminism*. New York: Pergamon Press, 1990.

Li An. "Congshu 'Qishi niandai hou'" (Reshape the post-seventies), *Furong* (Hibiscus), no. 4 (1999): 8–9.

"Li Dawei vs. Wei Hui: Gei suo juzhu de chengshi tushang yiceng fenhong se" (Li Dawei vs. Wei Hui: apply some pink color to the city we live). 15 September 2004. http://edu.sina.com.cn/wander/2000-09-15/12271. shtml (accessed January 10, 2005).

Li Dazhao. "Spring," trans. Claudia Pozzana. *Positions* 3 (Fall 1995), 306–327.

Li Gan, Xiong Jialiang and Cai Shuxian, ed. *Zhongguo dangdai wenxueshi* (History of contemporary Chinese literature). Beijing: Kexue chubanshe, 2004.

Li Jiefei. *Chengshi xiangkuang* (The city frame). Taiyuan: Shangxi Jiaoyu chubanshe, 1999.

Li Jingze. "Bei zhebi de qishi niandai ren" (The hidden 70s generation). *Nanfang wentan* (Southern literary forum), no. 4 (2000): 49–51.

Li, Xiaojang. *Guanyu nüren de dawen* (Answers about women). Nanjing: Jangsu renming chubanshe. 1997.

——. *Xiawa de tansuo* (Eve's exploration). Zhengzhou: Henan renmin chubanshe. 1988.

Li Youliang. *Gei nanren mingming: ershi shiji nüxing wenxue zhong nanquan pipan yishi de liubian* (To name men: ideological evolution of criticizing the patriarchal ideology in the 20th century female literature). Beijing: Shehui kexue wenxian chuban she. 2005.

Li Zhengliang. "Pingmian meiti de shehui shenfen xiangxiang yu 'yulun daoxiang' de dacheng" (The imagination of the social identity in the media and the achievement of media guidance. http://hermes.hrc.ntu.edu.tw/csa/journal/27/journal-park211.htm (accessed December 26, 2004).

——. "Taipei, Shanghai he Zhongguo xiaozi" (Taipei, Shanghai and Chinese petit bourgeoisie). http://www.srcs.nctu.edu.tw/CSA2005/papers/0108-A1-1-Li.pdf (accessed December 10, 2004).

"Liang Dong yu Muzi Mei duihua" (Liang Dong interviews Muzi Mei). 4 December 2003. http:// big5. phoenixtv.com:82/ gate/big5/ www.phoenixtv.com/home/sms/renwu/200312/04/158111.html (accessed October 20, 2005).

Link, Perry, Richard P. Madsen, and Paul G. Pickowicz, eds. *Popular China: Unofficial Culture in a Globalizing Society*. Lanham, MO: Rowman & Littlefield Publishers, 2002.

Liu, Jianmei. *Revolution Plus Love: Literary History, Women's Bodies, and Thematic Repetition in Twentieth-Century Chinese Fiction.* Honolulu: University of Hawai'i Press, 2003.

Liu Kang. "Is There an Alternative to (Capitalist) Globalization? The Debate about Modernity in China." In *The Culture of Globalization,* ed. Fredric Jameson and Masao Miyoshi, Durham, NC.: Duke University Press, 1998. 164–188.

——. "The Internet in China: Emergent Cultural Formations and Contradictions." In *Globalization and Cultural Trends in China.* Honolulu: University of Hawai'i Press, 2004. 127–161.

Louie, Kam. *Theorizing Chinese Masculinity: Society and Gender in China.* Cambridge: Cambridge University Press, 2002.

Lu Jie, "Cultural Invention and Cultural Intervention: Reading Chinese Urban Fiction of the Nineties." *Modern Chinese Literature and Culture* 13, no. 1 (Spring 2001):107–139.

——. "Rewriting Beijing: A Spectacular City in Qiu Huadong's Urban Fiction," *Journal of Contemporary China* 13, no. 39 (2004): 323-338.

Lu, Sheldon. *China, Transnational Visuality, Global Postmodernity.* Stanford, CA.: Stanford University Press, 2001.

Lu Tonglin. *Misogyny, Cultural Nihilism, and Oppositional Politics: Contemporary Chinese Experimental Fictions.* Standford, CA.: Stanford University Press, 1995.

Ma Li. "Shenghuo zai ai'lin" (Live in Ailin). *Xiaoshuo jie* (Fiction world) 5, (1998): 118–121, 136.

MaCracken, Ellen. *Decoding Women's Magazines: From Mademoiselle to Ms.* New York: St. Martin's Press, 1993.

Mallan, Kerry and Sharyn Pearce, ed. *Youth Cultures: Texts, Images, and Identities.* Westport: Praeger, 2003.

Mao Jian. "Xiaozi shi zenyang liancheng de" (How petit bourgeoisie is tempered). http://www.culstudies.com/asp/list2.asp?id=1375&writer=maojian (accessed December 30, 2004).

Mao Zedong. "Militia women." In *The Poems of Mao Tse-tung,* trans. Willis Barnstone and Ko Ching-po. New York: Harper & Row, 1972. 99.

Man, Eva Kit Waah. "Female Bodily Aesthetics, Politics, and Feminine Ideals of Beauty in China." In *Beauty Matters,* ed. Peg Zeglin Brand. Bloomington: Indiana University Press, 2000. 169–196.

Mattelart, Michèle. *Women, Media, and Crisis: Femininity and Disorder.* London: Comedia Pub. Group, 1986.

——. "Women and the Cultural Industries." *Media, Culture and Society* 4 (1982):133–151.

Mattews, J.J. "Building the Body Beautiful." *Australian Feminist Studies* 5 (Summer 1987): 17–34.

McRobbie, Angela. *Feminism and Youth Culture*. New York: Routledge, 2000.

——. "Shut up and Dance: Youth Culture and Changing Modes of Femininity." *Cultural Studies* 7, no. 3 (1993): 406–426.

Meng Jinwei. "Shangye baozhuang cuisheng 'meinü zuojia'" (Commercial packaging produces "beauty writers"). 27 October 2000. http://edu.sina.com.cn/literature/4/627.html (accessed June 23, 2003).

Meng Yue and Dai Jinhua. *Fuchu lishi dibiao: xiandai funü wenxue yanjiu* (Emerging from the horizon of history: study on modern women's literature). Beijing: Zhongguo renming daxue chubanshe, 2004.

Mengzi. *Mencius*, trans. James Legge. http://www.sacred-texts.com/cfu/menc/menc22.htm (accessed October 22, 2005).

Meyers, Marian, ed. *Mediated Women: Representations in Popular Culture*. Cresskill, NJ: Hampton Press, 1999.

Mian Mian. *Tang* (Candy). Beijing: Zhongguo xiju chubanshe, 2000.

——. *Candy*. Trans., Andrea Lingenfelter. Boston: Little, Brown. 2003.

——. Baise zai baise zhi shang (White above white). Beijing: Qunyan chubanshe, 2005.

——. *Shejiao Wu* (Social dance). Beijing: Xin shijie chubanshe, 2002.

——. *Xiongmao* (Panda sex). Beijing: Qunyan chubanshe, 2004.

——. "Yige bingren" (One patient). *Furong* (Hibiscus) 4 (1999), 34–36.

——. "Zhe yichang 'meinü zuojia' de naoju" (The farce of "beauty writers"). sina.com.cn/literature/celebrity/shows/4/824.html.

"Mian Mian reaches maturity with 'Panda Sex,'" *China Daily*, 1 March 2005. http://www.chinadaily.com.cn/english/doc/2005-03/01/content-420714.htm.

"Mian Mian: jiejin wuxian touming de hongse" (Mian Mian: getting close to the endlessly transparent red). http://www.dragonsource.com/tuijian/mianmian.htm (accessed November 11, 2004).

"Mian Mian jiedong zhihou tuichu shejiao wu" (Mian Mian wrote *Social Dance* after the ban is lifted). 16 May 2002. http://cul.sina.com.cn/s/2002-05-16/12826.html (accessed November 11, 2004).

"Mian Mian: jiuge mubiao de yuwang" (Mian Mian: nine objects of desire). 26 October 2003. http://she.563.cn/article/2003/2003-10-26/606.html (accessed December 12, 2004).

"Mian Mian yi paidui de mingyi shenghuo" (Mian Mian lives in the name of party). *Jingping gouwu zhinan* (A guide of smart shopping), 11 July 2004. http://www.92china.com/Htmls/Consumed/nblife/20040711210133.htm (accessed November 11, 2004).

"Mian Mian zibai: xiezuo de 'shenti xing' bushi yuwang" (Mian Mian's confession: body writing is not desire). http://www.booker. com.cn/ gb/paper54 /1/ class005400034/ hwz103339.htm (accessed October 22, 2005).

Muzi Mei. *Yiqing Shu–Riji Quanbanben* (*Ashes of Love: complete Diary*). Beijing: Er shi yi shiji chubanshe, 2003.

"Neirong gediao dixia de 'meinü wenxue' bei jing." ("Beauty literature" with low-grade content and taste was banned). 15 June 2000. http://edu.sina.com.cn/wander/2000-06-15/4584.shtml (accessed February 20, 2005).

Ng, Janet. *The Experience of Modernity: Chinese Autobiography of the Early Twentieth Century.* Ann Arbor: University of Michigan Press, 2003.

Oswell, David. "A Question of Belonging: Television, Youth and the omestic." In *Cool Places: Geographies of Youth Cultures,* ed. Tracey Skelton and Gill Valentine. London: Routledge, 1997. 35–49.

Peng Jianze ed. *Meiti jianfei shipu/xiaozi shenghuo shipu* (Recipes of beautifying bodies and losing weight /petit bourgeoisie's Recipes). Changsha: Hunan renming chubanshe,1998.

Perreault, Jeanne Martha. *Writing Selves: Contemporary Feminist Autography.* Minneapolis: University of Minnesota Press, 1995.

Pomfret, John. "A New Gloss on Freedom: Sexual Revolution Sweeps China's Urban Youth." *Washington Post,* 6 December 2003, final edition.

Pozzana, Claudia. "Spring, Temporality, and History in Li Da Zhao." *Positions* 3 (Fall 1995): 283–305.

Qi Shuyu. *Shichang jingji ia de Zhongguo wenxue yishu* (The art of Chinese literature in the market economy). Beijing: Beijing daxue chubanshe, 1998.

Qiu Huadong. "Xin meiren" (New beauty). In *Yaogun Beijing* (Rock'n'roll in Beijing). Beijing: Zhongguo wenlian chuban gongsi, 1998. 371–382.

Robertson, Roland. "Glocalization: Time-Space and Homogeneity-Heterogeneity." In *Global Modernities,* ed. Mike Featherstone, Scott Lash and Roland Robertson. London: Sage, 1995. 24–44.

Robin, Kevin. "Cyberspace and the World We Live in." In *Cyberspace/Cyberbodies/Cyberpunk,* ed. Mike Featherstone and Roger Burrow. London: Sage, 1995. 136–155.

Sang, Tze-lan D. *The Emerging Lesbian: Female Same-Sex Desire in Modern China.* Chicago: The University of Chicago Press, 2003.

Sassen, Saskia. *The global city: New York, London, Tokyo.* Princeton: Princeton University Press, 2001.

Schiebinger, Londa, ed. *Feminism and the Body.* New York: Oxford University Press, 2000.

Selected Works of Mao Tse-Tung, vol. 1. Beijing: Foreign Language Press, 1964

Sha, Jichai, ed. *Dangdai Zhongguo Funü diwei* (The status of contemporary Chinese women). Beijing: Beijing daxue chubanshe, 1995.

Shao Yanjun. *Qingxie de wenxuechang* (The unbalanced literary field). Nanjing: Jiangsu renming chubanshe, 2003.

——. *"Meinü wenxue" xianxiang yanjiu: cong "70 hou" dao "80 hou."* (Research on the "beauty literature" phenomenon: from "post-seventies" to "post-eighties"). Guiling: Guangxi shifan daxue chubanshe, 2005.

"Shei jiao wo meinü zuojia wojiu gen shei guobuqu" (I am not happy at those who call me a beauty writer).http://www.booker.com.cn/ gb/paper54/1/class005400034/hwz103335.htm (accessed December 12, 2004).

"Shenti xiezuo yu xingwei yishu: Muzi Mei, Jiu Dan, Wei Hui, Mian Mian, Chunshu" (Body writing and performaning arts: Muzi Mei, Jiu Dan, Wei Hui and Mian Mian). 12 August 2004. http://www.culstudies.com/rendanews/displaynews.asp?id=3414 (accessed October 20, 2005).

Sherman, Barrie and Phil Judkins. *Glimpses of Heaven, Visions of Hell: Visual Reality and Its Implications*. London: Hodder and Stoughton, 1992.

Shi, Anbin. "Body Writing and Corporeal Feminism: Reconstructing Gender Identity in Contemporary China." In *A Comparative Approach to Redefining Chinese-ness in the Era of Globalization*. Lewiston: Mellen Press, 2003. 129–206.

Shi Jianghu. http://www.wenxue2000.com/.

Shi Zhanjun. "Gaobie xinsheng dai" (Farewell, new generation). *Xiaoshuo pinglun*, no. 3 (2001): 92–93.

Shu Shu. "Di sanjie Lu Xun wenxue jiang gongbu, '70 hou' zuojia shoujin zhuliu" (The third Lu Xun Literary Award announced, and "post–seventies" writer mainstreamed for the first time). 29 December 2004. http://www.chinanews.com.cn/news/2004/2004-12-29/26/522273. shtml (accessed November 10, 2005).

Skelton, Tracey and Gill Valentine, ed. *Places: Geographies of Youth Culture*. London: Routledge, 1998.

Smith, Marc A. and Peter Kollock, eds. *Communities in Cyberspace*. New York: Routledge, 1999.

Sontag, Susan. *Illness as Metaphor and AIDS and Its Metaphors*. London: Penguin, 1991.

"Stefan Landsberger's Chinese Propaganda Poster Pages." http://www.iisg.nl/ ~landsberger/iron.html.

Ta Ai. *Shi MeinüZuojia Pipanshu* (Criticizing ten beauty writers). Beijing: Hualing chubanshe, 2005.

Tang Xiaobing. "In Search of the Real City: Cinematic Representations of Beijing and the Politics of Vision." *Chinese Modern: the Heroic and the Quotidian*. Durham, NC.: Duke University Press, 2000. 245–272.

Templin, Charlotte. *Feminism and the Politics of Literary Reputation*. Lawrence: University Press of Kansas, 1995.

Todd, Richard. *Consuming Fictions: The Booker Prize in Britain Today*. London: Bloomsbury, 1996.

Tseëlon, Efrat. *The Masque of Femininity: the Presentation of Woman in Everyday Life*.London: SAGE, 1995.

Wang Anyi.*Chang hen ge* (The song of everlasting sorrow). Beijing: Zuojia chubanshe, 1996.

Wang, Fei. "Literary Calls from Women Novelists." In *Feminism/Femininity in Chinese Literature*, ed. Peng-hisang Chen and Whitney Crothers Dilley, 187–98. Amsterdam: Rodopi, 2002.

Wang Meng. *Wang Meng xuanji* (Selected works of Wang Meng). Tianjin: Baihua wenyi chubanshe, 1984.

Wang Jing. *High Culture Fever*. Berkeley: University of California Press, 1996.

——. "Youth Culture, Music, and Cell phone Branding in China." *Global Media and Communication* 1, no. 2 (2005): 185–201.

——. "Bourgeois Bohemians in China? Neo-Tribes and the Urban Imaginary." *China Quarterly*, no. 183 (September, 2005): 532–548.

Wang Shuo. *Playing for Thrills*. Tr. H. Goldblatt. New York: William Morrow, 1998.

——. *Please Don't Call Me Human*. Tr. Howard Goldblatt. New York: Hyperion East, 2000.

——*Wanzhu* (Master of mischief). Nanjing: Jiangsu wenyi chubanshe, 2005.

Wang, Zheng. Women in the Chinese Enlightenment: Oral and Textual Histories. Berkeley: University of California Press, 1999.

"Wenxue wangzhan fazhan: wangluo wenxue zouxiang guimohua fazhan" (The development of literature website: Internet literature becomes formal). http://www.chinahtml.com/management/4/2006/gren-11428150143 956. shtml.

Wei Hui. *Shanghai baobei* (Shanghai baby). Shenyang: Chunfeng wenyi chubanshe, 1999.

——. *Shanghai Baby*. Trans., Bruce Humes. New York: Pocket Books, 2001.

——. "Wo haixiang zenme ne?" (What else do I want). *Zuojia* (Writer) (July 1998): 25.

——. *Shuizhong de chunü* (A virgin in the water). Shijiazhuang: huashen wenyi chubanshe, 2000.

——. *Wo de can* (Marrying buddha). Shanghai: Shanghai wenyi chubanshe, 2004.

"Wei Hui he Zhang Yuan de duihua: xiangle zhuyi zhe de 'linghun show'" (the dialogue between Wei Hui and Zhang Yuan: "the soul show" of the hedonists). 29 September 2004. http://culture.china.com/zh-cn/reading/writer/11022791/20040929/11898679-1.html (accessed January 15, 2005).

"Wei Hui de zitai he Mian Mian de shengming" (Wei Hui's attitude and Mian Mian's announcement). 14 Aprile 2000. http://www.white-collar.net/wx—wxf/wxf04/161.htm (accessed January 8, 2005).

"Wei Hui fangtan" (An interview with Wei Hui). http://www.54youth.com.cn/gb/paper107/zt/xyzt/WH04.htm (accessed February 20, 2005).

"Wei Hui he *Shanghai Baobei*" (Wei Hui and *Shanghai Baby*). http://edu.sina.com.cn/2000-05-05/5/33.html (accessed April 4, 2005).

Wei Wei. "Yige nianling de xing yishi" (Sexual consciousness at different ages). *Xiaoshuo jie*, no 5 (1997): 165—168.

——. "Chong xie chengyu gushi: dui xiaoshuo de yidian lixiang" (Rewriting idiom stories: a little idealism for novels). *Furong* (Hibiscus), no. 4 (1999): 38.

——. "Cong Nanjing shifa" (Starting from Nanjing). *Zuojia* (Writer) (July 1998): 98—110.

——. "Da Lao Zheng de nüren" (Old Big Zheng's woman). *Renming wenxue* (People's literature), no. 4 (2003): 59—70.

Wei Wei and Zhu Wenying. "Xiezuo, yinxiang he neixin huodong" (Writing, impression and mental activity). *Zuojia zazhi* (Writer magazine) 4, 2003. http://www.writermagazine.com/2003/4/xie.htm (accessed October 6, 2004).

Weitz, Rose. *The Politics of Women's Bodies: Sexuality, Appearance, and Behavior.* New York: Oxford University Press, 1998.

Whelehan, Imelda. "Sex and the Single Girl: Helen Fielding, Erica Jong and Helen Gurley Brown: for the English Association." In *Contemporary British Women* Writers, ed. Emma Parker. Woodbridge: Brewer, 2004. 28—40.

Widmer, Ellen and Kang-i Sun Chang, eds. *Writing Women in Late Imperial China.* Stanford, CA.: Stanford University Press, 1997.

Wolf, Naomi. *The Beauty Myth: How Images of Beauty Are Used against Women.* New York: W. Morrow, 1991.

Wolmark, Jenny, ed. *Cybersexualities: A Reader on Feminist Theory Cyborgs and Cyberspace.* Edinburgh: Edinburgh University Press, 1999.

Wood, Robin. "Images and Women." In *Issues in Feminist Film Criticism*, ed. Patricia Erens. Bloomington: Indiana University Press, 1990. 337—352.

Worthington, Marjorie. "Bodies That Natter: Virtual Translations and Transmissions of the Physical." *Critique: Studies in Contemporary Fiction* 43:2 (2002 Winter), 192–208.

"Writers Born in the 1970s Stimulate Debate." *China Daily*, 20 October 2004. http://www.chinadaily.com.cn/english/doc/2004-10/20/content-384079.htm (accessed October 24, 2004).

Wu Liang. "Zhe yidai ren de shenghuo he xiezuo" (Life and writing of this generation). *Xiaoshuo jie* (Fiction world) 2, (1997): 180–182.

Xiao Jianhua. "Guanyu Wei Hui he Mian Mian deng 'qishi niandai hou' zuojiade sikao" (Thoughts on 'post-seventies' writers such as Wei Hui and Mian Mian). *Wenhua yanjiu* (Culture studies), 9 November 2004. http://www.culstudies.com/rendanews/displaynews.asp?id=4040 (accessed January 15, 2005).

Xiao Xue, ed. *Xiaozi fengqing: kangnaixin xiandai nüxing shenghuo xiaobaike* (Petit bourgeois's taste: carnation modern women's life encyclopedia). Nanjing: Nanjing chubanshe, 2003.

Xie Youshun. *Huayu de dexing* (The virtue of the discourse). Haikou: Hainan chubanshe, 2002.

——. *Shenti Xiuci* (Body rhetoric). Guangzhou: Huacheng chubanshe, 2003.

Xing Xiaofang. "Yipi nianqing nü zuojia zhanlu toujiao" (A group of young female writers stand out). *Zuojia* (Writer) (July 1998), back inside cover.

Yang, Mayfair Mei-hui. ed. *Spaces of Their Own: Women's Public Sphere in Transnational China*. Minneapolis: University of Minnesota Press, 1999.

——."Mass Media and Transnational Subjectivity in Shanghai: Notes on (Re)Cosmopolitanism in a Chinese Metropolis." In *Ungrounded Empires: The Cultural Politics of Modern Chinese Transnationalism*, ed. Aihwa Ong and Don Nonini. New York: Routledge, 1997. 287–319.

Yang, Xiaoyan. "Huashuo dutu shidai–Li Tuo, Liu He zhuanfang," (Talks on image-reading era–interview Li Tuo and Liu He), 30 May 2005. http://www.cul-studies.com/community/lituo/200505/1995.html (accessed November 10, 2005).

Yang Ke, ed. *2000 nian Zhongguo xinshi nianjian* (Yearbook of New Chinese Poem in 2000). Guangzhou: Guangzhou chubanshe, 2001.

Yin Lichuan. "Weishenme bu zai shufu yidian" (Why not be more comfortable). 31 January 2000. http://www.wenxue2000.com/poet/ylc.htm (accessed September 20, 2005).

Yi Wen. "Wangluo jiushi richang shenghuo: Zhou Jieru tan wangluo." (Internet is daily life: Zhou Jieru talks about the Internet). http://culture.netbig.com/topic/935/20000605/29011.htm (accessed December 29, 2004).

"Yong pifu xiezuo yong shenti jianyue nanren" (Using my body to inspect men and my skin to write). 13 October 1999. http://users.cgiforme.com/leoxl/messages/84.html (accessed November 14, 2004).

"Yong shenti xiezuo: nü xieshou fabiao xingai riji" (Writing with the body: female writing staff publishes sex diary). 12 November 2003. http://www.people.com.cn/GB/shenghuo/1092/2184434.html (accessed September 12, 2005).

Yu Hua. "One King of Reality." Tr. Jeanne Tai. In *Running Wild: New Chinese Writers*, ed. David Der-wei Wang. New York: Columbia University Press, 1994. 21–68.

"Zhang Ailing: cainü haishi meinü?" (Zhang Ailing: beauty or literary woman). 1 November 2000. http://culture.163.com/edit/001101/001101-42778.html (accessed June 23, 2003).

Zhang Lin, "'Xiandaihua' yujing zhong de 90 niandai wenxue zhuanxin" (The transformation of literature of the 90s in the context of "modernity"). *Ershi yi shiji* (the 21st century), no. 21 (December 2003), 31 December 2003, http://www.usc.cuhk.edu.hk/wk-wzdetails.asp?id=2823.

Zhang Xinxin, "How Did I Miss You." In *One Half of the Sky*, trans. R.A. Roberts and Angela Knox. New York: Dodd, Mead & Co., 1987. 92–124.

Zhang Xinyin. "Yu shenghuo xiang huying: huiwang 2003 nian duanpian xiaoshuo" (In concert with life: retrospection on novellas of 2003). *Wenxue bao*, 5 January 2004.http://www.news365.com.cn/wxpd/ds/rdjj/t20040105-6250.htm (accessed October 29, 2005).

Zhang Xudong. *Chinese Modernism in the Era of Reforms: Cultural Fever, Avant-garde Fiction, and the New Chinese Cinema*. Durham, NC.: Duke University Press, 1997.

Zhang, Yingjin. *The City in Modern Chinese Literature and Film: Configurations of Space, Time, and Gender*. Stanford, CA.: Stanford University Press, 1996.

Zhang Yiwu. *Cong xiandaixing dao houxiandaixing* (From Modernity to Postmodernity). Nanning: Guangxi jiaoyu chubanshe, 1997.

Zhang Zhe, "Xuezhe wei meinü zuojia 'haomai'" (Scholars feel the "pulse" of beauty writers). http://news.xinhuanet.com/book/2003-03/12/content-773258.htm.

Zhang Zhen. "Mediating Time: The 'Rice Bowl of Youth' in Fin de Siècle Urban China." *Public Culture* 12, no. 1 (2000 Winter): 93–113.

Zhang Zhizhong. *Jiushi niandai de wenxue ditu* (The map of literature in the 1990s). Taiyuan: Shangxi Jiaoyu chubanshe, 1999.

Zhao Bo. "Guanyu xing, yu sha sha tan xin" (About sex, confide with Sha Sha). *Xiaoshuo jie* (Fiction world), no. 6 (1997).

Zhao Jinhua. "Zuojia shangwang ganshenme" (What writers do on the Internet). http:// www.linlins.com/ NewMoon/2/ 2000-07-21-23-45-11.html (accessed December 14, 2004).

Zheng Guoqing. "Anni Baobei, 'xiaozi' wenhua yu wenxue changyu de bianhua" (Anni Baobei, "petit bourgeoisie" culture and the changing Literary field). *Dangdai zuojia pinlun* (Criticism of contemporary writers) 6 (2003): 74–79.

"Zhiming pinglunjia zuojia shuo Wei Hui" (Famous critics and writers comment on Wei Hui). 23 April 2000. http://edu.sina.com.cn/ critique/2000-04-23/2192.shtml (accessed February 6, 2005).

Zhongguo Funü (Women of China). Beijing: Zhongguo Funü chubanche, 1990–2002.

Zhou Jieru. *Xiao yao de wang* (Xiao Yao's net). Shenyang: Chunfeng wenyi chubanshe, 2000.

Zhou Xiaohong, ed. *Zhongguo zhongchan jieceng diaocha* (Investigating Chinese middle class). Beijing: Shehui Kexue wenxian chubanshe, 2005. http://book.sina.com.cn/nzt/fin/zhongguozhongchanjieceng/3.shtml (accessed February 2, 2006).

Zhu Wenying. "Dao Shanghai qu" (Go to Shanghai). *Xiaoshuo jie* 1 (1999): 156–162, 165.

Zhu, Aijun. *Feminism and Global Chineseness: The Cultural Production of Controversial Women Authors.* Youngstown, NY.: Cambria Press, 2007.

Zito, Angela and Tani E Barlow ed. *Body, Subject & Power in China.* Chicago: University of Chicago Press, 1994.

Zong Renfa, Shi Zhanjun and Li Jingze. "Guanyu 'qishi niandai ren' de duihua" (Conversation on "people born in the 70s"). *Changcheng* (Great Wall) (January 1999): 195–202.

Zuojia (Writer) (July 1998).

INDEX

Asian Thought and Culture

This series is designed to cover three inter-related projects:

- *Asian Classics Translation*, including those modern Asian works that have been generally accepted as "classics"
- *Asian and Comparative Philosophy and Religion*, including excellent and publishable Ph.D. dissertations, scholarly monographs, or collected essays
- *Asian Thought and Culture in a Broader Perspective*, covering exciting and publishable works in Asian culture, history, political and social thought, education, literature, music, fine arts, performing arts, martial arts, medicine, etc.

For additional information about this series or for the submission of manuscripts, please contact:

Peter Lang Publishing, Inc.
Acquisitions Department
29 Broadway, 18th floor
New York, New York 10006

To order other books in this series, please contact our Customer Service Department at:

800-770-LANG (within the U.S.)
(212) 647-7706 (outside the U.S.)
(212) 647-7707 FAX

Or browse online by series at:

www.peterlang.com